From A
Soddy

Compiled by

Marlys Miller Denholm

As told by
the late
Henry Miller
and others

From A Soddy

ISBN: 0991441788
ISBN-13: 978-0-9914417-8-5

Marlys Miller Denholm

CONTENTS

Part A

Part B

Part C

Epilogue

INTRODUCTION

Dear Reader,

From A Soddy was begun by my father, the late Henry Miller of Bristol, South Dakota. He was a small boy when his family moved from Pipestone, Minnesota, to homestead south of Lemmon, South Dakota. The family of six lived in a soddy, under the same roof as the livestock for more than a year before the frame house was built.

Millard and Sabilla (Gorter) Denholm, formerly of Webster, South Dakota, were friends of my parents, and so enjoyed my dad's stories that they encouraged him to start a book. My father fell ill with inoperable cancer in early 1968, and passed away April 16 of that year. He and Mother had thirteen chapters of *From A Soddy* fairly complete. Mother, Evelyn (Wampler) Miller, formerly of Hecla, South Dakota, gathered more information and wrote from notes she and my father had made. Mother passed away July 20, 1969.

Uncle Louie Miller and his wife, Clara (Hoefling) Miller, and Aunts Hilda (Miller) Baumeister and Alice (Miller) Holdal, and Uncle Don Miller, all formerly of Lemmon, South Dakota, were very generous with their time and storytelling abilities. Without their help, I could not have brought *From A Soddy* together. Without Louie's help, there would be no maps at all. Even though all of them are now deceased, I am indebted to them.

We have tried to preserve the speech mannerisms of my grandparents. Each incident is a true story. Many historical facts are worked into the conversations. Those who know the area and the family will know of things that could or should have been included, but under the circumstances this could hardly have been avoided.

It is my hope that we who enjoy this great state will have a better understanding of the joys, sorrows, and hardships experienced by the early and later pioneers who built South Dakota, and that you will enjoy reading *From A Soddy*.

Respectfully,

Marlys Miller Denholm

ABOUT DAD AND MOTHER

By Henry Miller

My dad, William Miller, was born April 8, 1869, near Hamburg, Germany. He came to the United States in 1883 with his father, Christoff Meuller, and an older sister and her husband. He was the youngest of the family, and his mother was buried in Germany. The family settled in Indiana and my dad worked as a farm hand. Later he joined the railroad crew and worked his way to Storm Lake, Iowa. There he met my mother, Carrie Lang, and married her in 1898.

My parents farmed near Cherokee, Iowa, before moving to Jasper, Minnesota, in 1902. In 1906, my dad went west and homesteaded the southwest quarter of section 11, DeWitte Township, Perkins County, South Dakota. Mother and we four children joined him the next year.

Dad spent the rest of his life in Perkins County, gradually building up quite a farming operation. During the drought and depression of the 1930s, he and Mother sold out to the Government. The land is now included in the National Grasslands.

They moved into Lemmon where they spent their remaining years. Dad enjoyed good health for some time, and he and Mother kept a cow, a team of horses, chickens, and a large garden, and Dad plowed gardens around town each spring. These were given up as years went on, but Dad continued to read and smoke his pipe by the stove. He kept up on politics and news. He still had a good voice and a full head of snow white hair at the time of his death in December of 1955.

Mother and Dad were married at Storm Lake, Iowa, on October 20, 1898, her eighteenth birthday. They lived in Buena Vista County, Iowa, where my brother Christoff was born in July 1899, and I in August of 1900. Mother was a tiny energetic person, barely five feet tall. She had bright blue eyes and long dark brown hair. This she wound into a knot at the back of her head. I don't think she ever had a haircut and she didn't get gray.

I moved my family from Perkins County to Day County, South Dakota, in 1948 and Mother made the trip by bus to visit us. After we moved to near Bristol along Highway 12, she rode with my brother Don in the truck and spent some time with us. I recall once in about 1952, that Mother, then past 70, rode with him and walked the short way to the buildings. The family was at school, so she found no one at the house. Mother set her things inside and set out to find me.

It wasn't long until she heard me moving around in the haymow. We weren't expecting company and I thought I was hearing things when she called, "Need any help up there?"

Mother loved people and she loved to talk; she would visit with anyone and everyone. Perhaps it was on this visit that Mother met our neighbor, Mrs. Kottke, who had come from Germany since World War II. Mother was disappointed that they couldn't visit in German. We have since learned that the modern language is based on Southern German while the family spoke the Northern language.

Mother passed away in May of 1960, after several years of failing health. Both our parents are buried in the Lemmon cemetery.

William Miller, 13 years old.
Picture taken the day he arrived in the
United States from Germany.

**William D. and Carrie (Lang) Miller
were married at Storm Lake, Iowa,
October 20, 1898.**

**Grandpa Henry Lang, Uncle Charlie Lang,
and Charlie's son, Lester Lang.**

From A Soddy

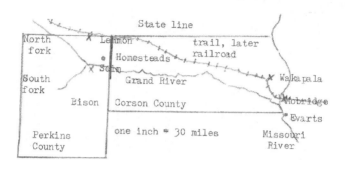

Old Evarts, South Dakota
Where Pa and company first crossed the Missouri by ferry in 1906. The railroad built north, and Evarts is no more.

Mobridge, South Dakota
Where the Chicago, Milwaukee St. Paul & Pacific Railroad built a pontoon and later a solid railroad bridge.

Wakapala, South Dakota
Where Pa and Uncle Charlie got off the train in 1906. End of the rails. They drove teams and livestock up the freight and cattle trail to the homestead south of Lemmon.

Seim, South Dakota (pronounced Sime)
Settled for the ranchers in the late 1880s. Located where the north and south forks of the Grand River meet, Seim once had a bank, postal station, stores, and land office. Pa and Uncle Charlie made claims from this land agent. Seim died out and the businessmen moved to Lemmon when the railroad came. State Highway 73 was built south of Lemmon in about 1916, and Seim reappeared as Shadehill. Today Shadehill includes a resort area called Summerville. Just west of the town lies the Shadehill Reservoir built in 1950.

Lemmon, South Dakota
Where the family got off the train in 1907 when we joined Pa on the homestead. Now a city of 2,400, serves a ranching area.

Bison, South Dakota
County seat since 1909, population some 460.

The Missouri River
Starting in Montana, the Missouri River meanders through west and central North Dakota, coming into South Dakota in the central north, and ambles south to Pierre, where it rambles eastward toward Sioux Falls and on south. The Missouri is the base of the Great Lakes of South Dakota.

The Grand River
The Grand River begins in two forks, one in North Dakota and one in central Perkins County, joining at the Shadehill Reservoir, and flows east to the Missouri River near Mobridge, South Dakota.

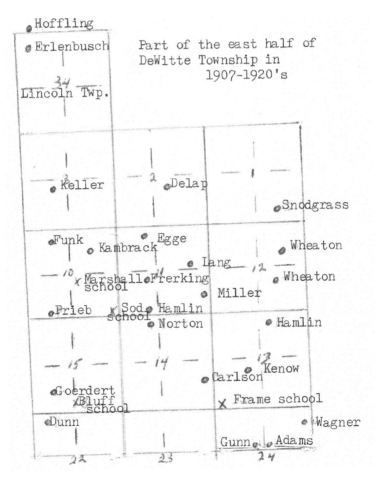

Reminder for the readers: As you begin the story told by Henry Miller, please remember that his remarks are relative to the time he worked on the book. When the text refers to "now" or "today", he is talking about late 1960s.

-Part A-

- 1 -
PLANS
SPRING, 1906

Chris and I jumped up and down. Our uncle was sticking bits of paper into two of his big finger nails. This meant a game of "Jack and Jill." Chris, or Christoff, was six, blond and curly haired. I, Henry or Hank, was five years old, about the same size with straight brown hair.

"Now stand over there," Uncle Charlie Lang said in German. He indicated the end of the table away from him. He laid the fingers with the bits of paper on the nails on the edge of the table. "Fly away Jack," our uncle said. Up went his hand and came down without the paper! As always, we stared in astonishment. "Fly away, Jill," and up went the other hand, to return to the table minus "Jill." We looked around our uncle's neck and collar for "Jack and Jill," never noticing how well hidden he kept his hands below the edge of the table. Uncle Charlie flicked his hands toward his ears and called, "Come back, Jack. Come back, Jill." The bits of paper were back!

"Tun es wieder!" we begged in German, "Do it again!"

Uncle Charlie shook his head, "We have grown-up talk now." Our Pa and Mother's brother, Charlie, had just returned from a trip to western South Dakota to look at land there. Several men had made the trip: a Mr. Wiesinger, a Mr. Sullivan, Uncle Charles Graffinteen, who was married to Mother's sister Anna, Grandpa Lang, and others. If we would sit quietly, we might hear the story.

"There's land just waiting for farmers to make something of it!" our pa said. Pa was short and fair, but well-muscled from his years of working on the railroad. "We can have a hundred-sixty acres just for living there and working it for a few years," he went on. His blue eyes snapped with excitement.

"There is a special rate on shipping stock for the homesteads," Uncle Charlie pointed out. Charlie Lang was a dark, kindly giant whom we children loved. Our uncle was a bachelor and we made the most of attention he'd have given his family, had he had one. "You can pay a dollar and a quarter an acre and own it now, too," he said.

Pa snorted, "Maybe you got two hundred dollars; I ain't. I got a family." He looked around, "There's an Ed Lemmon out there says there'll be a town coming up at the end of the railroad. That's where I want to get off the train! Way out where there's no one there." He turned to look at Mother, "Let's go, Carrie! I want to be a part of that new country!"

Mother didn't seem happy at the prospect, and Grandma Lang said quickly in German, "That land's not proved. Who knows what it really is like? Ach! So they raise cows; that won't mean you can farm it. Why, in parts of Germany they raised cows and goats but no crop, remember?" Grandma was a large woman and she spoke loudly.

Uncle Charlie unfolded a map put out by the railroad. "You get on here," he pointed out. "Then go to Madison, Bristol, and Roscoe in See Dakota. Then the train goes into Nee Dakota to Bismarck and this Glen Ullin." The grownups leaned over the map. "Or you can go to Evarts in See Dakota like we did."

"Why not go to Bismarck?" Grandma put in. "That sounds like a good German town."

"Why not Minnesota?" Grandpa asked. "You can't spend your whole life moving around."

"The train stops at Ullin?" Pa checked the map. "That's where I get off. I want to be at Lemmon's new town when the train gets there. I want to help settle the new country!" He smiled happily as though things were all settled.

"How about us?" Mother asked, "Did you ask me if I want to go to this Indian what-you-call-it place?" Mother was slim short and small boned. She was so used to looking up to talk to people that she tipped her chin to speak even to a child. The bun of dark hair at the back of her head bobbed indignantly.

"It used to be a reservation, Carrie," Uncle Charlie explained. "It isn't any more. They don't need it, so it's open to settlers."

The men returned to the map. "How far a haul from Glen Ullin?" Uncle Charlie wondered.

"Oh, maybe thirty or forty miles." Pa said. (It's about fifty as the "crow flies.") "We'll tie your wagon behind mine and you can ride a horse and drive the cattle along," Pa planned.

Grandpa laughed. "After a few days in a boxcar, you won't be able to drive them anywhere!" he said.

"Stop at Bismarck, and I'll come see you," Grandma put in stubbornly.

Pa ignored her, "Is it closer to haul from Evarts?"

Uncle Charlie studied the map. "This means a bridge of some kind," he pointed. "A pontoon at Bismarck and a ferry at Evarts in See Dakota. It's about the same distance afterward, but a shorter train ride, so less fare, see?"

"Yah, yah," Pa said.

"Now, where did you go and how?" Grandma asked.

"We went by train like this," our uncle traced the route from Pipestone, Minnesota, to Madison, Bristol, Roscoe and

Evarts in South Dakota. "Here at Evarts, we carried our things down to the ferry and helped pull it across the big Missouri River. The railroad ends at that river town."

"We get across and see some big wagons," Pa took up the story. "The freighters haul all the things that people out west need, like stoves, overalls, kerosene, and new saddles."

"We rode with the freight men to a little town called Seim and we looked at land," our uncle said. "The north and south branches of a river they call the Grand River come together there."

"And what did you decide?" Grandma needed to know.

Grandpa shook his head, "No."

"We are going," Pa told her and all of us. "Not right away, but we'll go. I filed for a quarter of land there."

Carrie Lang Miller with children, Hilda, Christoff, and Henry Miller, and Rose Graffenteen, a cousin, in 1905.

It was planting time now and nothing more was said about moving. We boys began school, both in first grade. It was common for children to go to school for a few weeks in the spring, then begin first grade again in the fall. School was a terrible experience for Chris and me! Our parents must have known we would have a language problem, but we weren't prepared for it. All we learned that spring was to hate school and to speak a bit of English.

Before harvest, Uncle Charlie and Pa began making plans for the move to the homesteads. Only young healthy animals would be taken; others would be sold to provide money for shipping fees. By working together, the men would manage with fewer horses and machines. Each would take four horses, four or six cows, tools, a walking plow, and a broadcast seeder. They took one hay rake and a mower for both farms, a set of sled runners, and a drag or harrow, one wagon and box, and one wagon with a hay-rack. A few household and personal items would complete their needs and make a train car load.

After harvest, Mother and we children were moved from the rented farm where Hilda had been born in 1903 and Louie 1905. We would live with Grandma and Grandpa Lang and their little girls, Tina and Mary, until Pa sent for us.

We all went to see the men leave by train from Pipestone. The loaded wagons were pulled onto flatcars and livestock loaded into cattle cars. Mother wept, something she rarely did, as she and Pa said goodbye. Chris and I stood with the hanging heads, and Hilda clung to Mother's long skirt. Grandmother must have kept little Louie with her; I never can remember his being there at the time.

"What if the Indians strike again, Bill?"

"Nien, nien, do not worry. Goodbye, I will send for you as soon as the train comes to Lemmon's town. Goodbye." Pa climbed into the cattle car before he could change his mind. From Grandpa's buggy, we saw the men wave as the train puffed out of Pipestone and headed north and west.

We began school with Mother's sisters, Mary and Tina, this time. It didn't take us long to decide we had it good before. We could speak and understand much English, but this teacher expected us to know the multiplication tables! A sharp rap on the knuckles with a wooden ruler was the penalty for a mistake. Many times we came home and showed black and blue fingers.

Grandpa helped us with the arithmetic and saved our hands more punishment. It was many years before I could forgive that teacher.

In the spring, maybe March of 1907, the letter with money for train tickets came from Pa. We were to be on the train the first part of April. Grandma was all upset. "Why you got to go way out there?" she demanded. "The end of the railroad, the end of the world! That wild man may not even be there," she grumbled. We had long known that Grandma didn't think much of our Pa's dreams, and she felt he was too old for her Carrie.

"Where a man makes a living, a woman makes a home," Mother snapped. "You taught me that."

Grandma sighed. "Wild Indians and crazy cowboys," she muttered. Grandma was almost right. Western South Dakota was quite wild and unsettled. Boom towns and scattered ranches was all there was. Later we would hear Miss Duncan tell how frightened the girls had been when some fellows were spoiling for a gun fight at a dance at Seim a year or so earlier.

"The baby buried here, too," Grandma fussed. We were only vaguely aware of the birth, death, and burial of tiny brother, Walter, who had been younger than Louie.

"I can't do no more for that boy," Mother said sharply, "I got to do what I can for the ones I have."

What a hustle and bustle as Mother and Grandma sorted through our things! Furniture was shipped ahead of us. There were things to store and things to go with us. Grandpa was grim those days. Fathers like to have their daughters near the safety of home. I think Grandpa enjoyed us, even though we filled his home to overflowing.

Finally we were on the way to our new home in a far wild land with the father we hadn't seen for half a year. We kissed Grandma and Grandpa and the aunts. Grandma cried and I saw the tears in Grandpa's eyes. Mother was brave, but it was a sad parting. We knew that our grandparents feared they would never see us again.

- 2 -
RECOLLECTIONS
APRIL, 1907

The novelty of the train ride was over and the boredom of the second day set in. I thought back to Pa talking of the wonders of the West. Grandpa had quietly favored the rich farmlands of Minnesota. Who was right? I thought of the past school term. It would be nice if there were no schools in South Dakota. I began to miss Mary and Tina. They were okay, and going to school had been better after we learned our multiplication. Would I see Grandpa's house again? That seemed more like home to me. Would I ever see dear Grandma and Grandpa again?

Last night we had stayed in a little town called Bristol. Here we changed from northbound to westbound trains and from passenger to immigrant travel. The immigrant train was a car hung on the end of a freight train. This car was less comfortable and chillier in the morning in spite of a coal stove stoked by the men. There were fewer windows for children to look out. We crossed a flat looking river. A passenger pointed out a boat to us and told us that this was the James River and the boat would go all the way to North Dakota. Where that was, we weren't sure.

Someone called out, "Aberdeen!" and the train stopped. "For coal and water for the engine," someone told us, but we couldn't see what would have been an interesting sight. We got off the train to use the outdoor toilet near the depot. In many smaller towns, we had gone to the bathroom behind the train. Little folks hid behind their mothers' wide skirts and grownups waited for a town with facilities. Many folks left the train; a few boarded, and we were on our way. Years later I learned that there was a college in Aberdeen when we were going out to live in a soddy!

My thoughts raced ahead to the place called Lemmon, to Pa who had gone last fall to prove up the land, the homestead, the new home for us all. Would we know Pa when we met? Would he know us? What would he say? Louie would cry; he hadn't see Pa since he was a baby and Pa would be just a strange man to him. Hilda was three. She didn't say much but I don't think she remembered Pa. Christoff and I hoped we would remember, but when you aren't quite seven and haven't seen someone for a long time, you don't know what to expect.

I must have slept after a while. The next time I looked out a window, a whole different landscape met my eyes. Below, I could see the gray water of a winding river. It looked like a wild country. Mother laid a sleeping Louie on the seat and took Hilda onto her lap so the little girl could see the town, hills, and river. I touched Chris's knee and startled him from sleep to see the sights. The town that was to become Mobridge slid into view. We saw a few shacks and soddies like all other western towns we'd passed. Here were log buildings from trees cut along the Missouri River. We had seen log buildings in Minnesota, they were nothing new.

The train stopped. Mother spied an outhouse not far from the tracks and hustled us in that direction. On our return we waited while the train crew took care of their business. More people got off the train and few or none got on. We were moving again. Slowly we rolled toward the river! There was high rough looking country on the other side. The engineer eased the train onto the "swing" bridge that spanned the Missouri. Would it hold the train? Men were talking of how the tracks sank under water on the pontoons when the train crossed. Once the engine and cars had passed, the bridge rose and floated again. "Ach, no wonder they called it a "No-bridge," Mother chuckled.

West of the river we chugged slowly up the hills. The landscape was bleak and treeless. We saw a few poor looking shacks and cone-shaped teepees. "Is this Indian country?" someone asked. Several men said it was. After a while, we saw a team and wagon carrying a number of people of all sizes. The horses were smaller and looked different from the large farm animals we were used to. They were more like our pony, Brownie. I looked at Chris and could see that he too wondered if these folks were indeed real Indians. I thought of Mother asking, "What if the Indians strike again?" and shuddered.

"Maybe some lunch would be nice," Mother suggested. She opened the box that she and Grandma had carefully packed. All that we would eat for the two day trip had been taken with us. Mother had the coffee jar filled at the hotel where we stayed the night. I carried it myself down the hill from the square hotel in Bristol to the depot, and Chris had carried the jar of fresh water. We used the water to cool the coffee. We ate hard cooked eggs from the box, though most folks today wouldn't eat a two-day-old egg.

We all asked for coffee with our bread and butter sandwiches. As a treat, Grandma had tucked some cookies far down in the box "for when they get tired." There must have been other foods, but this I remember.

Deep in the food box safely locked in a jar, was a ball of sponge or starter for Mother's bread baking. Sponge was a small portion of the bread dough saved each time a woman baked. Anyone who lost her sponge or let it come to harm had to borrow from a neighbor before she could make bread.

Most of the passengers on this last lap of our journey were men. Some tried to be friendly, but most of them didn't speak German, and Mother's English was very limited. We thought English was for school, and we weren't used to being interpreters. This was all new to us and to our Mother, and we were very shy before strangers. We were probably easy to look after, as we likely clung to Mother all the time.

One dark and wrinkled fellow grinned at us. I'm sure he meant to be friendly, but it was frightening. We rode along looking at the floor, lost in our private thoughts or dozing. Late in the afternoon a man came and spoke kindly to Mother. She nodded then hustled us into our jackets and gathered up caps and handed us each a small bag or box to carry us as we made ready to leave the train.

- 3 -
END OF THE LINE!

"Lemmon, the end of the line!"

We felt the train slow down and looking out the window, we could see only grassland. Soon a few small buildings appeared along with a couple of large tents. This was the railroad camp a few miles east of Lemmon. The train groaned to a stop and we made our way to the door. Mother quickly checked to see that nothing was forgotten. The dark man that had frightened us indicated he would carry the large awkward lunch box. Mother smiled and nodded but she kept an eye on him until the box was safe at her feet outside the train.

We stepped off the train almost into Pa's arms. He was smiling happily. Pa took a bag from Mother and hugged her. He set the bag down and turned his attention to us, patting our heads and looking us up and down. "Lang, tall, bick boys," he went from German to English and looked from one to the other of us. Our pa turned to Hilda and tweaked her hair, "How is my madchen?" he asked. He picked up Louie who began to cry and reach for Mother. "Well, yah, he take a while," Pa said cheerfully. He turned to Mother, put a strong arm around her. "Did you have a good trip? Tired? The boys gut help, yah? Hungry?" he went on in German.

"We ate, but something hot would be nice," Mother told him. Pa rubbed his hands together; he seemed very pleased. Maybe he had been afraid we wouldn't come.

"There's a good place to eat. Come load up now." We put boxes and bags into the farm wagon and looked around us in the dusk. The wind blew and tall grasses rustled. Cattle in pens near the tracks were restless.

Huge freight wagons stood nearby. "Knocken?" I whispered, "Bones?" What kind of place is it that has wagon loads of bones?

"Yah, bones," Pa had heard. "The settlers pick up loads of buffalo and cow bones. "They get two dollars a ton for them in town. The bones are put on the train and hauled east to a place that makes fertilizer."

The railroad workers were coming from the day's labor. Teams of horses and mules, men and equipment, Indians in blankets, and others dressed as the other workers filed past. "Sure a lot of horses," Chris grinned. Little did we dream that only a few years later Pa, Louie, and I would be building a road under much the same circumstances and along this same route!

Boxes, barrels, crates, and furniture stood along the railroad tracks. Here and there a stack of lumber waited to be hauled away and put to use. "Don't people take stuff set around like this?" Mother worried.

"Not much except for horse stealing," Pa told her. "Some of that lumber is ours," Pa pointed with his thumb. "We are going to have a wood floor." Mother looked startled, but before she could speak, Pa rushed on. "Charlie took one bed frame and the chest, and all the feather ticks, and your trunk."

This was important. The trunk held the folks' marriage papers and our baptismal records as well as any books we may have brought from school, and baby things for any future family. Mother nodded; that was safe.

"One bed?" Mother questioned, "We need at least two. No one is going to sleep on the floor with the mice and spiders."

"There's just one little bitty snake that wouldn't hurt no one," Pa teased, "and it's a nice soft dirt floor ..."

"Nein, nein! They say those dirt houses are full of mice. I should have brought a cat, too." She sounded grumpy but she was smiling.

"Mein Gott!" Pa exclaimed as the loading went on. "Do we need all this? Why, Charlie and I have been getting along just fine."

"It's different with children," Mother reminded him. "Can we leave things here like this?" she worried.

"Yah, yah," Pa said, "Charlie's coming for the hogs in a few days, and he can get your stuff then."

"Hogs?" Mother said, "And have my churn ride with hogs?"

"Ach! We'll put a gate in the wagon then," Pa's patience was wearing thin. "Yah, a guy is sending out a bunch of sows and I spoke for two so we can get some hogs started and raise some meat for my boys to grow on."

"Gut, gut," (good) Mother said in a tone that meant she was out-talked. "So Charlie took a bed; we'll take the other. Bring the bedding, the children will need to lie down. Get my sewing machine, I bet everything you guys own is full of holes."

Finally the load was ready for the long ride home. Mother took Louie in her lap and set Hilda up between her and Pa on the spring seat of the wagon. Christoff and I settled ourselves on the roll of bedding. Pa took up the lines and turned the big team westward along the new laid tracks. It was perhaps a mile to the town proper. A train loaded with ties, rails, and such supplies stood down the tracks west. We stared as we moved past the engine.

"How would you guys like to try that?" Pa asked. "They get a whole dollar a day and board to work the railroad. Them as have horses get another dollar for the use of the team." We looked this way and that. Pa didn't expect answers. "You know I built railroad until I got to Iowa? I have some sisters and brothers in Germany, but I was the only one left to home. My brothers couldn't leave 'til they served in the army there. I was too young when we left."

This sounded exciting and very far away. I remember seeing our Grandpa Christoff Mueller once. He spelled his name the old way and I'm not sure when our dad took the English spelling, perhaps when he married. Grandpa came to Minnesota for a few days, and then he returned east and none of us ever saw him again. My grandfather was a big fellow with a beard. Anyway he seemed big to a small boy.

"It cost a hundred-fifty American dollars to come to America," Pa went on. "Then if you didn't have some money left over, they put you on the ship back. Most went to Illinois and Indiana." Pa laughed. "They weren't so fussy when the Langs came. Your grandpa, he stowed away and sneaked in. Ha, ha, time they found him it was too late to turn back and they dared not throw him overboard!"

"The railroad is a good way to go west," Pa informed us. "But I want to farm, so when I got to Iowa I stayed. In the Old Country all the land belongs to the rich. Us, we have no chance. Here we can own land. We can be farming people!" he went on grandly.

I had decided I couldn't stand riding any longer when we sighted the town that was to become our new home. "Here it is," Pa said proudly, pulling up the team of horses. As the wagon came to a stop, we saw several square-front buildings and some sod houses. Chimneys of the sod buildings or those with sod roofs appeared to be extensions of the stovepipes inside. "Most of the lumber came by train to Glen Ullin in Nee Dakota. The rails ended there just like out where you got off the train. When we came, we got off at Wakapala. That was the end of the line. We came on one of the first trains that crossed the Missouri River!"

We drove into the town from the east. Main Street ran east and west in the early days. Pa pointed out business places as we came to them: the livery stable and feed store, Reasy's blacksmith shop, Payne's general store, and Bamble's hardware. "There's a hotel and bar over there, and a laundry," our pa pointed. We tried to see everything, but we were tired and confused and it was dark now.

"You know what? When they opened the hotel they had bags of hay for mattresses. And the hotel was a tent! That's real pioneering," Pa told us. "These are smart business men. They got all set up to be here when the trains come. There's talk of a dentist and a drug store. There's a school.

"Will the boys go to school there?" Mother asked wearily. School! I thought miserably.

"No, there's one out our way," Pa said. "How about some coffee?" He turned the team up to a small building. We were glad for the cheery lights in the windows. We walked to the door and Pa herded us inside. I sniffed and grinned. Hotcakes! I expected to eat my fill as I had often done at Grandma Lang's. "Coffee for my family," Pa called.

He seated us at a small table and pulled up a stool for himself. There were several men seated alone a counter. One of them said something to Pa and he pulled his stool over there where they visited in a mixture of German and English. A woman brought the coffee and Mother indicated she would like some water. The warmish, stale water tasted terrible, but it did cool the coffee. That tasted nothing like Mother's or Grandma's! Pa was back. "There's a fifteen mile ride yet," he tried to hurry us. "Charlie will be looking for us and I want to stop at the store."

Outside, Pa waved to a fellow across the street. "They came, Hunt, just like I said," he called. Mother looked as though she didn't care to be the subject of a guessing match between Pa and a friend. "Marshall Hunt," Pa explained.

We went into the store. Pa picked up a sack of flour, some dry fruit, tobacco, and a can of kerosene for use in the lamps. "Anything else?" he asked Mother. She shook her head. "I don't know what you got. It takes salt to make butter; have you sugar?" Pa picked up a couple more items.

We could hear tableware on dishes in the back room. The lady came into the store and spoke to Mother. "You haven't had supper yet, have you?" She looked sympathetically toward us children. "You are all so tired. We had a big pot of soup. I put it on to heat and there's lots of bread and coffee. Come in, you have a long ride yet."

How grateful we were to this kind lady! It wasn't like our pa to eat so quickly and talk so little, but he was in a hurry to be on the way.

When the foodstuffs were loaded, there was room for two to lie down and a third child to sit on a roll of bedding. Hilda snuggled into the quilts and Chris and I took turns sitting on the blankets rolled nearby. It was night as we began our long ride south and east. There was only a dim trail and we wondered how Pa knew where to drive.

"How you like to ride behind Buck and Prince again?" he asked of no one. "It'll take three hours with this big load. You can make it in two empty, and with a saddle horse in an hour." There wasn't a light or a farm to be seen. After awhile the moon rose big and beautiful on the horizon. What a welcome sight! How good to see something familiar as we listened to our parents talk of the homestead and soddy. We could see the lines of the hills and now each other.

"That sod house is snug and warm in winter and not too hot in summer. Lots of room for kids to grow, too." Pa looked around at us. "Charlie and I spent a comfortable winter. He stayed with me, but he has a house. Has to have one to prove up."

After a while, Pa said, "Carrie, there's something you should know about the house. It's - it's not all house." We stopped our dozing and daydreaming to listen. How could a house not be a house? "I built the house twenty-five by forty feet," Pa said sadly. "All neat and strong, a good house for my family, and a big house for a big family. A house for you and me and all our kids, I built." He sighed. "Then up in the hills it is so cold, and some have horses stolen. I don't have time to make another building, Carrie. So I make half the house into a - a stinking barn," he finished. No one spoke and Pa went on, "Some have a creek or the river bank or trees to protect stock in winter. I like this place; it is like the part of the Old Country. There are hills and grass and more hills, but no place to winter the stock."

Mother put a small hand on his arm, "It is not forever, Bill. We will have a big house one day. Is good enough. How big?"

"Two rooms and an alleyway with cows and horses on the other side. The house part is on the east with a door and three windows. You go outside to get to the barn." Pa brightened. "A creek runs north to south along the west side of our quarter. Is good place to water stock. There are plums and chokecherries along the creek." Our mother nodded. Stock water was very important, and the fruits would be good. "The same creek runs through Charlie's land. His is just north of ours," Pa said cheerfully. "Wait until you see Charlie's dugout!"

We looked at each other, wondering if we dared ask what a dugout was, but our parents with sleeping Louie stretched across both their laps were lost in their conversation. Hilda slept, and Christoff and I traded places. I crawled in with our sister and he sat up a while.

-4-

THE PRAIRIE HOME

"Whoa! There's your house, Mamas. What you think of it?" I came out of sleep with my head bumping Hilda's and then a box of foods. The train was awfully rough. Then I remembered I was in the farm wagon and that was Pa's voice. I was up in time to see Uncle Charlie open the door of our house. Lamp light spilled out the door and small window. Pa climbed down with the sleeping baby and Uncle Charlie helped mother down and hugged his sister. Then our favorite uncle helped us jump over the wagon sides and tousled our hair while mother studied her new home in the moonlight.

Pa watched her. "It's a good house," he said quickly, "just a little heat for cooking and it's all warmed up. Do you know what we burn? Buffalo chips, right off the prairie! There's wagon loads the boys can pick up. I got lots of little jobs for you boys. Come on in," he beckoned. We moved toward the house.

I realized that the house and the barn were indeed all one building! The west wall of the house served as the east wall of the barn. The two-foot thick sod wall would keep barn noises and odors from the family living quarters. Soon we would learn that there were doors on the south where hay was brought in, on the west where the stock went in, and on the east where we were about to enter.

We were still standing in the doorway when Pa returned from putting Louie on the bed and went for Hilda. We stepped into a room about twelve by fifteen feet. The walls were the dark colors of the sod; rafters of two-by-fours and small tree trunks held up a dark sod ceiling. The bark was peeled from trees and they shone pale in the yellow glow of the kerosene lamp on the table. The floor of earth was packed by Pa's and Uncle Charlie's feet over the winter they had lived in the soddy. Well, I thought, if someone spills it'll soak away and we won't have to wipe it up. How wrong was I! People even mopped these floors.

Only the cook stove, table, and a few chairs occupied the kitchen. Our Pa had pots and pans and his dishes in wooden boxes on chairs. There was a partial wall of sod with an open doorway between the kitchen and bedroom. In that room was a bed and Pa's box of clothing. The room was the same size and shape as the kitchen. I thought of the furniture in the wagons outside and wondered where we could put it.

Pa was back. "Have a drink of water and see how good it is. We have a real good well here. But we have to pull the water up by hand. Maybe next year we can get a pump." We drank from the enamel dipper in the pail on the table. More strange water! It would be a day or two before we learned that the water was hauled from a shallow, hand-dug well nearly a half-mile away, along the creek.

Mother had fit things into the house mentally. Now she said, "Come boys, and help us here." Back at the wagon, she handed us bags and boxes with instructions as to where each would go.

"We got our ten acres broke and Charlie's," Pa was saying. "Next year we'll break another ten or more."

The beds were set up with a loud banging that made the little folks cry. "Boys, get some rugs down," Mother shook her head. "Dirt floors, bah!"

"I want everything in," Mother told the men. "The air is damp, and I don't want my sewing machine wet. Put it under the kitchen window so I can see to sew."

"It don't rain all the time like Minnesota," Pa told her. "It could snow though, it's damp enough. In '05 they had a terrible snow in May; lost a lot of stock, even some folks that was out."

Pa and Uncle Charlie brought in the rest of the loads: the large chest with dishes, a second lamp, and garden seeds stuffed in with our meager wardrobes, a commode for the wash basin and water pail. In came a sort of box with shelves for Mother's dishes, now packed in towels, jackets, and the like to protect the few that were not sturdy enameled tin. Mother's sewing machine was brought in, its drawers stuffed full of patching, threads of different kinds, her precious scissor, needles, safety pins, and buttons which she saved from worn out articles of clothing.

Feeling "dog tired," I sat down on the nearest chair and thought about Ma's sewing machine. I must have been four years old when Pa went to an auction sale and came home proudly lugging a nearly new treadle sewing machine.

"There, Mamas," he exclaimed, "The next one won't have to wear hand-sewed things." He watched Mother for a reply. She was quite a tease, but she could take it as well.

For once, Mother didn't have a retort on the tip of her tongue. "Oh, Bill, you shouldn't have! They cost so much. Why, I can sew things by hand," she went on. Then, "How does it work?"

The lady had threaded the machine and showed Pa how to run it. "Sit down, I show you. Chris, give me your shirt." Pa had noticed a tear in the shoulder. Once Mother got onto the method of treadling, she stitched the tear quickly. We stood by, amazed at the noise and speed of the machine. We all began looking for a rip or tear for Mother to sew. The sewing machine became one of her most prized possessions. That machine sewed and mended for the nine of us who grew up. The old "Damascus" is still in my home and it still sews.

The sewing machine was probably of little consolation when the "next one" arrived. Pa was away and Mother was alone with three small children. Hilda was just two, I was five, and Christoff, six years old. That's worse than no help! Mother sent us out to play and said she would call us when she wanted us to come in. I don't know if Pa came home before she called or not. When we went into the house Mother was in bed with tiny new baby brother Louie.

When we were old enough to understand, we would know that it was considered quite something for a woman to be alone at this time and to take care of her newborn baby and herself. This is what our little mother had to do.

"Er schlafend?" the voice said. "He asleep?" Pa asked. I shook my head; they were talking about me! "Come help a little," Mother handed us things to set on the table. We ate quickly and Mother rushed off to make beds. "You'll stay, Charlie, and visit a bit." Anytime the family got together it was the custom to visit until two in the morning. Perhaps that began here.

Uncle Charlie must have stayed to hear the news of the family in Minnesota. First he told us about the storm cellar where Pa had said there was milk for breakfast. The cellar was a pit dug into the ground and covered. A tree trunk held up a roof of smaller branches or boards, then straw or grass with earth over that. Grass grew over the earthen covering and almost hid the shelter from view. Steps were cut into the wall on one side to make a stairs. There were doors at both top and bottom. Due to the heavy snows a flat door would not do at the top, so a little house was built there. It kept rain from running into the cellar, and it may have kept flies out in the summer and helped keep the cellar warm in the winter. The storm cellar was near the house since we had to go there often for food.

"It is a fine cool place in summer," Uncle Charlie went on, "your mama can keep the milk there and the eggs when we get some hens. It's a good place for potatoes and carrots and such things, too." Wisely he didn't tell us that time that the cellars were also protection against the occasional tornadoes that swept across the plains. "Some folks build them only half as deep and build a half-house on top to live in. But your papa, he builds a big house."

"When can we see your – er – house, Uncle Charlie?" Chris asked and I wondered if you call a dug-out a house.

"Not tonight, guys," our uncle chuckled. "You best be getting to bed."

"Jenny's a good cow," Pa remarked to Mother as she came into the kitchen. "She gives almost two gallons a milking. You can break in another one to have milk year-round for the kids." We knew that he considered milking women's work so we thought nothing of Mother breaking or training the cow. That's how it was in the Old Country, as Pa liked to call it.

"Soon as you get my crocks and churn, I'll skim cream and make some butter," Mother said. She suddenly asked, "Do you suppose there are folks in town would trade for butter?"

"We'll see," Pa said.

"I'm looking forward to some of your good bread, Carrie," my uncle said. "Living on pancakes and hardtack biscuits gets tiresome. Not all the time, mind you, but a loaf would be a treat."

"I sure can bake for you, Charlie," Mother said. "You get a sack of flour now and then, and I'll keep you in bread. Or maybe get me some baking fuel; I just don't know about these chip things you talk about." She looked hard at Pa. "You keep a house warm in winter with that?"

Mother set her flour barrel near the stove so the flour would be warm in the morning. She carefully unpacked the bread starter and stirred it into the warm potato water. Now she was all set to make a big batch of bread first thing in the morning. Chris and I grinned, if mother was baking, this was home.

"Last winter some folks burned twisted hay," Pa informed us. "Why did they twist it, Chris? Well, it's safer and easier to handle. But you have to stuff the stove all the time anyway." He turned to me, "Hank, you learn to chop wood yet?" I looked at the floor and shook my head. "Grandad didn't teach you? Well, we'll go down to the river one day and get a whole load for you guys to practice on."

Pa turned to Mother, "They say there's some light, dusty coal for the taking along the river east. I'll try to get some for the colder weather, come fall."

"You boys get to bed now," ordered Mother. "You'll be tired come morning, and there's lots needs doing." She sighed, "You'll have to be starting school. Pa says there's one opened last fall over past the creek." We sighed, too.

Chris and I made our trip outside wondering if there was a good sod outhouse somewhere in the chilly yard. If there wasn't, my mother would see to it that one was begun promptly in the morning. We could see the light from the small four-paned window on the south side of the kitchen. There was one like it on the east and one on the east wall of the bedroom. We would learn that the lack of north and west windows helped keep the soddy warm during the severe Dakota winters.

"How did Pa hang a door on the sod?" We found a sturdy wood frame set into thick sod wall. The door hung on three leather hinges.

"How about that, boys?" Pa asked. "And look at the ceiling, just a few pieces is all it takes to hold it up. It's a good thing we don't have lots of rain, or might wash the roof down. We can cover the sod with some lumber before summer." Our Pa was pleased and proud of his work.

"It's spring, better get busy. Where's that lumber?" Mother put in. The grownups laughed and Pa motioned with his thumb towards the bedroom. We went.

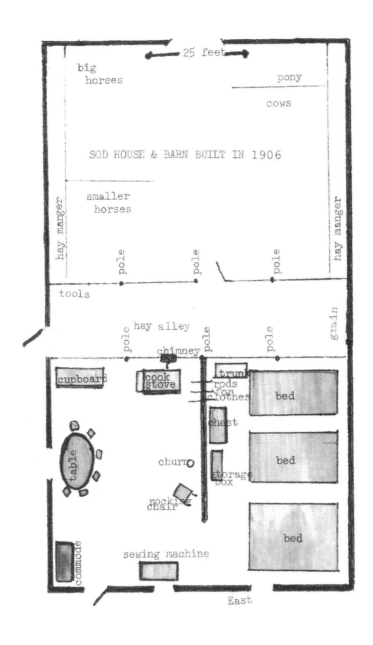

-5-
LIFE IN THE SODDY

We renewed friendships with Pa, Uncle Charlie, and the stock we had known in Minnesota. We missed Mother's big German shepherd, Jack, who had been left at Grandpa's.

Pa did have a lot of little jobs for us, and some not so little. While our uncle made the all-day trip to the railroad for the sows and the rest of our belongings, we boys and Pa fixed a pig pen and shelter of some kind for the animals. This must have been of lumber because hogs would have torn down a sod structure in no time. "They got to have shade," Pa explained. "Some guys from the Old Country don't know how strong the sun is here and they let the hogs get too hot and die."

We learned that the much talked about "chips" are nothing more that sun-dried cow and buffalo droppings, and that picking them up is work, not a game. We all rode along on the stone boat to the creek to get a barrel of water for use at the house. Stone boats are home-made sleds built for hauling things that are too heavy or awkward to load on a wagon. There are a number of planks or split logs laid across a pair of heavy runners or skids and nailed down. A chain is fastened to the ends of the runners, and a double tree or evener is fastened to the middle of that chain. This is the mechanism by which the horses pull the load. You can ride standing if you are careful, sitting if you don't mind getting dirty, or sit on a turned over pail as Mother liked to. This way we could be shown the farm and pasture lands.

Mother was happy about the fruit trees along the creek, just as Pa had hoped. While we rode along, Pa pointed out where our boundary lay, where the muskrats were for wintertime trapping, or where we could pick up buffalo bones to sell to "help us get on our feet."

"Whas das?" Mother pointed off to the left. We looked in time to see some white patches bobbing away. Pa laughed, "They're antelope, sort of a deer or wild goat. They are wild, but good to eat."

Mother was enjoying the trip. She was really a farmer girl and she and Pa talked of the good land for crops and the hilly sections to be fenced for pasture.

"The school is over there," Pa pointed south and west. "Soon you go. The school is a deserted claim shanty. They call it the Marshall house because the guy's name was Mr. Marshall. Up there in the high hills there are coyotes." He pointed across the creek and a little south. "One night soon we'll hear them howl." In time, we were home with a two or three day supply of water and some education as to our surroundings.

One day Uncle Charlie came in his wagon to take us to his home. "You got to finish your chores first," Mother reminded us. It was our chore to bring in wood each evening for the night and next day, but with Uncle Charlie's help we soon had a great stack of wood next to the range. We filled a box with small wood for fire starting in the morning and emptied the pail of waste water outside. We hauled in water from the barrel to fill the pail in the kitchen.

"Does your mama need her lamps filled?" our uncle asked. We didn't know. "Well, ask her quick," he said. So Uncle Charlie showed us how to fill the bowls with kerosene. Mother quickly said she'd clean the chimneys, thin glass globes that she washed and dried with the dishes. Uncle Charlie helped us pour the oil and clean the outsides of the lamps. He reminded us not to spill because our papa had to buy that oil and it cost money.

"Here Carrie," our uncle said when we went inside, "the boys can do that for you right along." We had another job! We weren't getting to Uncle Charlie's and I began to feel grumpy.

"Have a bite now," Mother said as she set out mugs of milk, fresh cinnamon rolls, and homemade butter. While we lunched, she wrapped a couple loaves of bread for Uncle Charlie to take home.

Then we were on our way over the green hills to see the great dugout. We drove north from our house a quarter-mile or more. We could have walked, but this was more fun. We talked and laughed as we rode behind our uncle's team.

"There it is," our uncle pointed to the south of a steep slope a short distance away. Our eyes followed his finger, expecting to see a dark form like our own home. There was nothing there! We looked at each other and at our uncle. He was grinning and chuckling. "I live in that hill," he told us.

Sure enough, there was half a house sticking out of the hill! As we neared the home site, we saw a stovepipe chimney on a grassy roof, two short wooden walls, each with a tiny window, and on the south a door like at home. Uncle Charlie stopped the wagon and we jumped down and ran to have a better look. "Man!" Chris exclaimed, "A house in a hill!"

I had visions of the house running back into the hill and maybe as big as ours inside. Uncle Charlie opened the door, "Come on in," he invited. Eagerly we stepped into a room of ten by ten or so feet.

Near the door was a tiny stove, farther back a small table and two chairs. A narrow cot with a feather tick on it stood against the back wall. At the foot of the bed was a wooden box that held clothing. A saddle straddled the box. Across from the table was a low cupboard on which sat a water pail with an enamel dipper like at home and at Grandma's house. The ceiling was just a little taller than our uncle and it sloped down toward the door and down toward the bed.

"Well, by the looks on your faces, I'm sure glad I'm not bringing a wife here," our uncle observed. We made haste to recover our manners. "H-how did you make it, Uncle Charlie?" I stammered.

"It's little – er, small and ah, nice," Chris put in.

Our uncle roared with laughter and we relaxed. "Well, you find a steep slope and a good shovel," he told us. "You measure a little and start digging. After you get a good sized hole, you can build up the outside walls with sod, or you can use lumber. Lumber houses have sod around the bottom to keep them warm anyway. Some guy up north ran into a nest of rattlesnakes when he was digging."

We went outside to look around. "Where's the barn?" Chris asked. We followed our uncle around the hill and down into a deep ravine, called a "draw" in the area. "Right here," Our uncle pointed to a thicket of short bushy trees. There was some fence and a sort of open, two-sided shelter built into the grove of small trees. Was he fooling us? Not this time. "My horses and few cows can find shelter down there. I keep only a little grain, just a few sacks in the house. Don't tell your mama, but we had grain in the bedroom at your house last winter."

We laughed, picturing what our mother would say. Of course we'd tell her; Uncle Charlie knew we would. It didn't matter. She would be finding kernels sprouting if Pa hadn't done a good job sweeping. Grain sacks have a way of leaking.

We ate dinner with Uncle Charlie. It was a meal of coffee, Mother's bread, and rabbit cooked with onions and potatoes. Our uncle told us about the winter in the west, the cold, the snow, and the coyotes. We talked about the shanty he planned to get and how he hoped to build a pole shed into the hillside. Late in the afternoon we walked the short way home fairly bursting with things to tell Mother and Hilda.

One of the first nights after we came to Perkins County, Pa called us all outside. "You want to hear something?"

Out we went, asking, "What? What?"

"Be quiet and listen." Pa commanded. We stood quietly, then a few quick barks followed by a long quavering howl came from the southwest. We jumped and grabbed at our parents.

"A wolf!" Mother said, "A crazy wild animal!"

Pa chuckled, "No, just a coyote. Now listen for another." Before he finished speaking, we heard the barks and the long howl from the north. Then a coyote howled east of the farm. "Come inside," Pa said, "and we'll talk about them."

We returned to the warm, bright soddy. Mother said, "And the boys got to walk to school! Wish we'd brought Jack. Ach, I don't like it a bit."

Pa pointed to the chairs and said, "Sit down, I'll tell you. They are like a middle-sized dog," he began. "You won't see them in daytime much. They aren't dangerous unless you have one in a trap or pick up a pup. The coyotes may watch you from the hills, but they won't come down in daylight. When you see one, you'll see he's sort of grey-yellow, maybe brown. His ears stand up and he has a bushy tail."

"What do they eat?" Christoff wondered.

"Gophers, rats, lots of rabbits," Pa said.

"They take turns chasing a rabbit. One starts then howls and another takes over 'til the rabbit is caught. Coyotes will eat a dead cow or calf. A bunch can get together and kill a sick calf or antelope. They're bad in sheep country."

"How far away are they?" I asked. They had sounded awfully close.

"That range of hills west is three-quarters of a mile. There is at least one den there. The first coyote we heard was along the creek this side of the hills. Some may live in the brush by the creek, they hunt there. There are a lot of them in the range of hills a few miles north. Some folks are hunting and trying to get rid of the coyotes. But they are nothing to worry about or be afraid of if you use head," Pa finished.

"Now," Pa said one morning at breakfast, "you know where our boundaries are and how the land lays, I want you to take the stock to the creek for water then herd them and while you watch, you gather up the bones you find. Get all of them. Make piles not too small and close, but so you don't have to carry too far. One day we'll take the wagon and gather up the piles of bones to sell."

"Ah, nein," Mother objected, "Boys should in school, Bill."

"Too late," Pa said. "School be out in a couple weeks. They can go in the fall."

"What now? School is out?" she countered.

"Out as soon as spring work starts," Pa said.

"Today the sun is warm. Christoff, where will the snakes be?"

"In the sun, Pa."

"And where will you walk then?" Pa turned to me.

"In the shade of a rock or a bush," I recited.

"Good, and on a hot day where will the snake be and where will you walk?"

"We walk on the hot side and the snake lies in the shade, Pa."

Outdoors, we were boosted onto gentle Brownie's back. "Don't pick the hill where the coyote den is," Pa said. "There may be a nest of pups and a fighty mother."

This looked like a lot of fun to us. The cattle had soon been watered at the creek and they spread out to graze. We had only to keep them from straying onto other homesteaders' acreages. This wasn't much of a problem as most land wasn't taken. We piled up bones, scouted the area, mounted and dismounted many times.

One of us would ride Brownie and the other would walk, picking up the bones the rider spotted. We changed off from time to time.

When the sun was high and we were hungry, we gathered the stock and moved nearer home. During the noon meal, Pa asked how we had gotten along.

"Did you get the bones?" If we had, we should move to a new area for the afternoon. So began our work as herd boys - work that would go for years to come.

One morning Uncle Charlie drove up with his big team of horses hitched to a hayrack. "Are you ready?" he asked as I stepped out of the barn

"Yah," I said right away. I didn't know what was going to be done, but if Uncle Charlie was going, I was ready. Pa came leading his big horses and Chris followed with a saddled Brownie. Chris let the cattle out of the corral, mounted Brownie, and moved southward with our stock and Uncle Charlie's. Pa loaded his saw, chain, and ax, and hitched the team to a wagon.

Now I knew we were going to the river for wood. We moved right along the two miles to the high bluff on the north side of the Grand River. In some places, there are trails to get up and down the bluff.

Pa drove to one such place and carefully eased the team and wagon down the narrow, twisting trail. Uncle Charlie followed, and Chris left the cattle at the top of the hill to graze. He coaxed Brownie down the steep hill. We drove past the Erickson's homestead and toward the river. It is a quarter- or a half-mile from the bluff. The Grand River was still high from spring flooding and there were a lot of logs and trash washed up on the banks. We boys were instructed to load the wagon with small branches. Pa and our uncle set about sawing up some larger wood. The work went on all forenoon.

Once Pa sent Chris to check on the cattle. I had begun to think we were staying all day when the men picked up tools and made ready to go.

At home we unloaded the wood and ate of Mother's good home cooking. Then we made another trip to the river. Pa told us to bring the stock down for water this time. "You want to ride?" Christoff generously let me use the pony and he walked as we herded the animals down to the river and back up the hill.

We were both riding Brownie down the steep slope when we met Pa and our uncle coming up. Each team of horses pulled a huge log. The logs were left at the top of the bluff. Once the wagons were drawn up the hill, the logs were chained behind them and dragged home. This wood would be sawed and split into stove-size chunks when the men had time. Pa looked pleased once the wood was unloaded and piled ln the yard. "That should last 'til after haying, maybe even past grain cutting if Mamas burns lots of cow chips," he predicted.

The crop on homestead land was usually corn, hand planted in the sod on the ten acres a man was required to plow that first year. This was no bumper crop, but there was hopefully some corn for the family's use. The stalks were cut with a knife, tied into bundles using a stalk for twine, and later fed to stock. Pa planted oats on his first plowing and corn on the new ten acres. I expect that others did the same. The broadcast seeder was hung on the end of the wagon, grain was shoveled into the hopper as the wagon moved. A chain around the axle powered the fan at the bottom, causing seeds to be broadcast in a circle behind the wagon.

Plowing and planting a vegetable garden followed the planting of oats. A spot was chosen north of the house and remained the garden for the many years the family lived there. Corn planting followed in late May or early June. Corn was planted by hand and both our parents were in a hurry to get the farm into full production, so there may well have been more than the second ten acres to plant, weed and hoe.

Hoeing and weeding were not such jobs as they sound as there were very few weeds in the early years. Weeds were brought in with seed grains and farming has a way of encouraging them.

Hay was cut from the tall prairie grasses with a noisy, horse-drawn machine. Then a hay rake, pulled by lighter horses would go out and make trip after trip across the mown field. Every so often the driver would press a lever that caused the long curved teeth of the rake to dump out their load of hay. The hay was dumped to form a long low pile called a windrow. In a day or two the windrows of hay were raked again into little piles called doodles.

Then a man and a boy would come with a hay rack, a large box on a wagon frame, and load the hay by hand with pitch forks. The hay was hauled and unloaded into a stack near the barn. This would be winter feed for cattle. Horses got some, but most often they dug through the snow for the dry brown grass during the winter.

The family had the custom of sitting outside the house on the cool east side after supper during the summer months. This was the time to visit with Pa or to hear the things he felt we should know. One evening in the early summer Chris asked, "How did you get this land?" Then came the story of Pa's first trip to the west. He must have told Mother on his return, but now the story began for us.

"The government sent the army in to survey. The surveyors measured this land into quarter sections, blocks of land half a mile each way. There are four quarters in a section of land, see?" We nodded whether we saw or not.

"Well, we took the train to Evarts," Pa went on. "That's ten or so miles south of Mobridge where you crossed the big river, remember?" We remembered well. "That was last year, and there was no bridge like now at Mobridge. We got off the train and carried our things down to the river and got on a sort of boat called a ferry. The ferry was fastened by a cable so it couldn't go downstream. We helped get it across the river. On the other side there were a lot of big freight wagons like the ones in town. We helped load the freight and the drivers offered us a ride west."

"Why didn't you come like we did?" I asked in German. All home conversations at this time were in German.

"Well," Pa went on, "the railroad men decided they couldn't make a bridge at Evarts, so they took up the rails and went north into Mobridge where you crossed." (Evarts died the death of so many towns missed by the rails.)

Pa said, "The freighters hauled everything the settlers and ranchers bought. There was flour and food stuffs in one wagon, coal oil (kerosene), tools, and a crate of new overalls on another, lumber, yard goods and a new cook stove on the next, and so on. There were the Phillips, Duncan, and Lemmon ranches here years before the rest of us came. And there were ranches along the Moreau River south for a long time. We learned that from the freight men."

"There was no town of Lemmon then, but the freighters came to the town of Seim over west a few miles. One day we'll go there for some reason and you can see it. It's near the river where the north and south parts meet. Now it's time for bed," he said. "I'll tell you more another time."

A few days later, we boys came from scraping the supper scraps to the hogs and found our pa and uncle smoking their pipes on the shady east side of the house. I took the plate in to Mother and we both quietly joined the men. After a few minutes, Pa said, "Looking for the rest of that story?"

"Yah," we nodded.

"Well, now we were at Seim, right?" We nodded again, and Uncle Charlie knew which story was being told. "There was a land agent at Seim and he took a wagon load of men around the country side to see what land they'd like. Over east of Seim a few miles, the country is hilly and lots of grass grows. It looks good to me. The agent says, 'what piece are you interested in?' and I say 'the west' because I want this piece with water on it."

The agent, we were told, had a map that showed high hills, creeks and cutbanks where the ground had caved away leaving small cliffs. Some places there were piles of rocks set up as landmarks. When the agent figured they were in about the right spot, he'd stop the team and the men would get out and look for a cement marker that the survey crew had set into the ground. When the marker was found, the man tied a red hanky on the wagon wheel and asked them to count the turns of the wheel. At a certain number of turns, there should be another marker. The prospective settlers climbed out to find that marker.

"So now I know that my quarter runs from this marker to that one and this way and back," Pa swung his arm showing us the large square of land.

"Then we took a stick and tied a rag on it and pounded it into about the middle of the quarter section," Uncle Charlie said. "And rode almost into Nee Dakota and filed there."

Pa laughed. "And we come home and say, 'We filed a claim there.' And Mamas and Grossma, they scold like everything! And in the spring when we came with the cows and horses, we had to get off at Wakapala because that's as far as the train went. You remember when we left?"

"Yah," Christoff said. "Mama cried, and the train had wagons on."

"You rode with the cows," I said.

"It's cheaper," Uncle Charlie told us. "Then when we got here we built the houses, first yours, then mine."

As the summer wore on, one or the other of us boys often went to help with haying, garden work, or weeding corn, and the other would herd the few cattle alone with the brown pony.

All of a sudden we were out following the hay mower in the oat field, one of as boys helping tie the bundles of grain. Sometimes we worked with Mother and some of the time with Uncle Charlie. Pa always ran the mower. When Mother went out we looked after the little folks at the house or in the field. The bundles were tied with a straw for a string, hauled to the barn to be fed to milk cows and hogs in the winter.

This still rather green oats was the only grain the cows would get unless we had some unplanned source of income and Pa could buy a bit of grain. Twenty or so acres of oats doesn't sound like much, but harvesting it in this way was a lot of work.

The summer of 1907 went quickly for us, as summers do for small boys. We had picked up bones, ridden our pony, and learned to herd cattle. We had been introduced to field work, gathered wood for Mother, as well as chips, and we learned about the rattlesnakes and where to watch for them. That's not quite right; you always watch, but some places you watch more carefully than in others.

We were fascinated by the dress and actions of the cowboys in this time when some still wore guns, mostly just to show off. But we rarely saw any neighbors. About the time of my birthday, August 30, Pa announced that our uncle would look after the cattle, and we were all going to town. This would be the first time for us children since moving west.

Mother fixed a lunch to take, spread a quilt over clean hay in the back of the wagon, and made sure each little person had a cap or sun bonnet. The fifteen-mile trip would be hard enough without getting sunburned. With great excitement, we washed up and put on clean overalls. Pa took his corn knife to be sharpened at the smithy. Mother's trading butter was carefully packed in a large pot. Jars of cold water from the cellar would help to keep it solid. Mother covered the pot with hay in the wagon bed and we were on our way.

"We need paper and pencils, and some number books," Mother planned. She mentioned foods she needed for her family and some things that Uncle Charlie had asked her to get for him. She had written to the family in Minnesota and that letter would be mailed.

Mother never read or wrote English. She had attended a German United Brethren school in Iowa through the sixth grade. Her letters home would have been written in German.

There were a few more settlers along the way to Lemmon, and the area looked friendlier than on the night we had made the trip out to our home. In the spring, the hills had been green, but even in good years, the grass is brown by August. We drove along on the wagon trail, over the range of hills to the north, and past a prairie dog town. Pa pointed out some fields and farms and a couple small herds of farm cattle or horses. No large farms or ranches were there between us and Lemmon.

Part of Lemmon's Main Street, 1907.

How much brighter and larger the town looked to us now! As I recall, the street ran east and west, maybe half a mile south of where the railroad tracks run now. The livery barn, or one of them, faced south just north of where the petrified wood park is now. There was no park then. Other businesses ranged up and down the street.

We stopped at the post office where Pa mailed the letter while Mother fumed, "We got to get this butter to the store right away!" There were newspapers from Pipestone, Minnesota, a bundle of weekly papers sent once a month and maybe some other mail. We didn't get much mail on this trip because Pa or Uncle Charlie had been into Lemmon perhaps once a month.

The store must have been our next stop. Mother traded her butter for sugar or something else we couldn't raise. Pa began a bargain in which a yearling calf would be traded for our winter supply of coffee and flour.

This bargaining would go on the next time he was in town and finally an agreement would be made. The butcher would have fresh beef for his town customers and we would have groceries. Pa could have gotten more for a larger animal, but we didn't have a two-year-old steer. This type of trading later included eggs, and it was carried on for years. The folks always called shopping "trading."

While Mother looked at fabrics, at something like three cents a yard, we boys and Pa made a trip to the smithy. What an impressive and exciting place that was! We stared and listened as Mr. Reasy and his helper sharpened tools, traded gossip with our pa, shod a horse, and cracked jokes with the bystanders.

This was a gathering place for men, and boys were seen and not heard. I don't recall that anyone spoke to us. We could hardly tear ourselves away when Pa left. He had to help Mother if she were to buy anything. Remember, she spoke very little English and didn't carry any money.

-6-
FALL AND WINTER, 1907

"School starts next week," Pa said at supper.

Sunday evening we were given haircuts and bathed. Chambray shirts and clean blue overalls were laid out for morning. Mother gathered our Minnesota books, and laid them along with our new pencils and papers. Two syrup pails with handles became lunch boxes, and we were ready for school.

"I'll take you this first time, that's all," Pa said. We went in the farm wagon. The school was well over a mile away, across the crooked creek that ran west of the farm and farther southwest. This was the deserted claim shanty, known as the Marshall House.

We carried our lunches of plain sandwiches and maybe a cookie in a syrup or lard pail. Everyone carried their own drinking water or went without. Each family furnished their own books until 1914. We had little pencils with pointed erasers and tan or grey tablet paper with real wood slivers in it.

Christoff and I had already been in two schools, but we were started as first graders anyway. In our new school we found ourselves feeling more kindly toward teachers in general. We made friends among the neighborhood children, and though we might have pretended not to, we enjoyed school. The morning walks to school took us in the direction of the sun, but as autumn wore on, those homeward treks into the northwest became harder and colder! Long scarves around our faces helped, but even then we walked backward to warm our poor noses and foreheads.

One Saturday, Uncle Charlie took us, along with a spade and a number of small animal traps, on a long ride along the creek and out to some nearby ponds where he showed us how to trap the muskrats.

Muskrats build a mound of mud, sticks and grass out in a marshy lowland. The mound is hollow inside, and there is a sort of shelf where the rats live. A hole in the floor leads right into the water, and the rats swim from mound to mound under the ice.

"Whoa!" our uncle called to his team. "Okay, boys bring the spade and let's see what we can do here." We all climbed out of the wagon and headed across the ice toward the rat mounds. Uncle Charlie took the spade and tapped around here and there near the base of the mound. Then with a sharp jab, he broke through the hard covering.

There was some angry chattering and a splash from within as the surprised muskrats hastily left their home. The inside of the plug Uncle Charlie had removed was wet, and the mound smelled strongly of muskrat. That is somewhat like skunk, only not so much. "Phee," I grumbled. "Are you sure it's worth it?"

Uncle Charlie set one of the traps. "For a nickel a pelt? You bet, that's good money!" He got down on his knee and reached into the mound. "I'll just set this on the shelf there, and we'll see what happens."

Our uncle carefully replaced the plug of mud he had removed and stuck a stick through the ring at the end of the trap chain that hung outside. "So the rat can't get away with the trap," Chris figured.

"You didn't bait it. What will they eat?" I asked.

"Roots that grow under the water," Uncle Charlie explained. "They are just dumb enough to stick a foot in the traps. You couldn't trap coyotes like that, huh?" We laughed. We'd heard how almost no one was clever enough to trap coyotes with any luck.

From A Soddy

"If you boys can check these traps along here on your way from school, I'll give you the pelts you get. Be careful to plug up the mound so the wind doesn't blow in and freeze up the water, and don't get any fingers in the traps."

The lesson went on and we learned to set traps using one foot to hold the spring while we set the trigger mechanism. Uncle Charlie set the rest of his traps up and down the creek. He who got there first trapped or grazed any unclaimed land. "In the morning we'll check the traps and I'll show you how to get a rat out," Uncle Charlie said.

Come morning, we learned trapping wasn't all fun. The foot-long furry animals that hadn't drowned came out of the mounds fighting and biting at the traps when we pulled on the chains. Uncle Charlie calmly swatted each rat on the head with a stick, then removed the body from the trap and tossed it into the wagon. "Think you can do that?"

"Ah-h, yes-s," we debated, thinking of the nickel pelt.

"Good, now let's see you set this trap and plug up the mound." Once that was done, our uncle handed Chris the stick and we moved on to the next mound. Soon we had shown that we could handle a few traps. Not all the traps caught rats, not all the rats stayed caught, and sometimes a coyote opened the mounds and kept the rats frightened away or swiped them from the traps.

Still, we learned and got started on a money-making project that would stand us in good stead for years.

One evening, Uncle Charlie said, "I'm going into town. What do you want with your money?"

"Candy?" I asked, thinking of the sensible things I should have mentioned.

"Some for Hilda and Louie, too?" our favorite uncle asked.

"Yah," we agreed.

Uncle Charlie brought the candy as well as new socks for us. I doubt if our few pelts brought enough money, but he made us think so. Cold weather came next and so much snow that the men took up the traps while they could still find them. We missed school more and more often.

"I remember a man in Iowa," Mother would say. "He went just to feed the stock, but it was blizzarding and he didn't come back. The family hoped he was safe in the barn, but no one dared go and see. After the storm stopped, someone went out, but they didn't find the man. Then the dog sniffed and barked at a place in the snow. Pretty soon they got a shovel and dug there." We had heard the story every winter since we could remember, but we listened for the fearful result just the same. "Sitting there, hunched up in a snow bank sat the old man, froze to death," Mother concluded.

On stormy days, we stayed home and played with the younger children or helped with harness mending or the repair of some piece of furniture. Sometimes we helped Mother tear worn out garments into strips for rug rags or cut quilt pieces for her. The day would pass pleasantly while the wind howled and the snow flew by the small windows and piled into drifts around the buildings.

The lumber hauled by team and wagon from the railroad was used for patching and laying a wood floor in the bedroom. The boards were simply laid side by side over the earth, and a couple more nailed across the ends to keep the floor boards from sliding around. We laid rugs on this to keep from getting slivers in our bare feet. The winter of 1907 was spent with a sod floor in the kitchen part of the house. Mother broke open the wooden boxes that foodstuffs came in and tried to cover the floor for a little more warmth or a little less dampness. She laid rag rugs here and there, but there weren't enough to cover two twelve-by-fifteen-foot floors.

Early in the winter, one chilly, windy afternoon, we came in to find Mother pushing sort of a putty into cracks where she could feel a draft.

The homemade putty was made of old newspapers soaked in water and cooked along with a little flour. This mixture hardened much like plaster; it wasn't pretty but it did fill cracks.

"Maybe we can just put papers over all the walls like some do," Mother said to everyone and no one. "I'll wait a bit and see if theirs stays up. Sticking paper to dirt!" In time our walls were covered first with thin muslin, then with newspapers, the same as most of the soddies and homestead shanties up and down the West River area.

Shortly before Christmas, we came from school one day to see Pa and Uncle Charlie unloading wood from the bobsled. Mother was poking around amongst the branches and picking out several which she laid aside. Next she took one and then another and stood them up in the snow. Mother studied her branches.

Finally, she tossed all but one back onto the wood pile. The one branch was carried to the house. We boys trailed along wondering what good - or bad - was to come of this.

The next time we saw Mother's branch, it had become a Christmas tree. Not a green, living tree, but a Christmas tree none the less, and the kind we would have for several years to come. To make our Christmas tree, Mother had set the branch into a can or pail of dirt. Then she carefully wrapped the smaller branches with colored cloth from her rug rags or with leftovers from sewing. The very few colored pictures from magazines or catalogues were saved and cut into tree or star shapes to be hung on our tree. This, with the four- or five-inch tag of cloth hanging at the ends of the branches, was our Christmas tree.

We probably had jackrabbit or antelope for Christmas dinner. We surely didn't get a lot of toys, but Mother would manage to have some socks or a shirt for us. Even in the hardest years, we had a box of apples. We had some packages, and we felt our first Christmas on the homestead a success.

-7-
SECOND YEAR
SPRING, 1908

Winter lasts longer in northern Dakota than in southern Minnesota.

Mother hadn't been off the farm since before Thanksgiving. Pa and Uncle Charlie had gone to town once or twice, but it was not fit weather for little folks to take a long ride in a bobsled. Someone must keep the fire going and be home when we boys returned from school. So Mother stayed home and baked bread, mended overalls, kept house in two rooms for six people, and tried to keep cheerful with only four-year-old Hilda for female company for months.

One morning, Pa sniffed the air and called "Chinook!" This meant that the warm south wind was melting the snow. But spring is an on-again, off-again thing in the northern states. We would have a few nice days and then more wintery weather. We found our creek running deep when we came to cross it on our way home from school. We wet our feet in the icy water crossing. Mother insisted that we ride Brownie until the creek went down. When the snow was gone from the hills and the creek was down, we walked again.

One of the glories of springtime in hilly country is the crocus, pasque, or May flower, they are all the same, a brave and beautiful lavender prairie flower. I have seen them come as early as April first and as late as mid-May, the difference being when the snow is gone. Clumps of the plants cling to the grassy hillside, the tall flowers waving in the chilly spring winds.

One evening we were coming around the house from the barn when a loud bang met our ears. "The river's breaking up!" Pa said happily. "It's spring for sure." Inside, he told Mother.

"It's what?" she pondered.

"The ice," Pa explained. "The ice breaks up on the Grand River south. The water starts to run over it when the snow melts, and then the river ice melts and big chunks like a stove come loose. They bang together and smash against trees and the river bank. Come out and listen!" We went outside to hear the ice. On a still night we could hear the popping and banging as the ice broke up with the spring thaw. For many days we would hear the roar of the rushing waters two miles south of the farm.

The kitchen floor began to give us trouble. You remember that our sod floor was covered with the flat parts of wooden boxes. This made a fine hiding and hatching place for spiders and crickets. Mother had us boys take out the boxes and break them up for fire wood. The floor must have been damp, because Christoff moved the wood box behind the stove and hollered, "Hey, there's a great green alligator under it!" His alligator was a lizard, right there in the house. We didn't know whether to run and look or run and hide. Mother had us take the rugs out and shake them. Then we hung them on the clothes line and beat them with a broom. The next good drying day, Mother would wash them by hand and hang them in the wind.

Pa got a roof of boards over the sod one before spring rains came. We laid a floor in the kitchen before summer. This was boards laid on two-by-fours and was much better than the floor in the bedroom. We enjoyed walking about and hearing the hollow thumps of our boots.

New buildings were the coming thing, and the fathers got together before spring work began and planned a school for their children. The new sod building was built not far from the Marshall House and we watched its progress on our way to and from school. The building was sixteen-by-twenty-four feet on the outside, and somewhat smaller inside. Doors and windows were set into the thick sod walls. The sod school was a fine building with shingled roof and lumber running up the peaks from the doorway.

The summer of 1908 was much like the one before for us, I expect. We herded cattle, helped with haying, milked cows, and being a year bigger and older, took on a larger share of the family work.

One morning, Pa asked if we were good milkers.

"Nein, no need," Mother said.

Pa looked hard at her. "Boys got to learn to milk," he said. "We come here to good land almost free to those who will work. And we will all have to work. If we don't want that, I might as well a stayed in the Old Country and never own an acre! All boys got to milk cows," he concluded.

"Yah," Mother sniffed, "I see how you like to milk."

Pa argued, "In the Old Country, no man milks, but here boys milk." We had long heard how in Germany, the girls and women did all the dairy work and how they washed the cows and white washed the barn walls until it was about as clean as the house.

The next morning after breakfast, Pa left to help Uncle Charlie with his barn and we boys carried milk pails along with Mother around to the north door into the barn. The cows were brought in from the fenced night pasture. "Redkins is gentle," Mother said. She sat down and brushed straw and dust from the cow's udder, then milked in long steady streams like we had often seen her do. "Now watch," Mother instructed, "you squeeze the top fingers first, then the next and on down, all the time pull just a little." She made room for Chris beside her.

He had only a little luck. Then I tried with about the same success. Mother sat on the short, one-legged stool, pushed her long skirt out of the way, and quickly finished the cow. "You can try again tonight," she said. "And remember how I say to work your hands, practice that." In a week we were milking Redkins.

When Mother's favorite cow, the white-faced Jenny came fresh, Mother milked her a few times then let Chris take over. Our mother checked the cows to see that the job was well finished lest the cow get a swollen udder or dry up from not being properly emptied at each milking.

One evening, Mother was in the garden when we came with the cattle. "You boys get started," she called. Chris milked the pet Jenny and I milked Redkins who wasn't giving much. Then we dared each other to milk the third cow.

"Ma's coming," I protested.

"Let's surprise her," Christoff coaxed.

"No, I'm taking this to the cellar," I left the barn with my pail. I found clean crocks and cloth strainer and strained the milk into the crock. I climbed the steps with skimmed milk for the calves.

My brother was milking the last cow and grinning fit to burst. I fed calves and carried more milk down stairs. This time I brought skim milk for the piglets.

By now Chris was done with the cow. "We finished?" I asked. We looked around, "Calves are fed, hogs are fed, cows out." We gave the calves a bit of hay and left.

Mother came into the house almost on our heels, "Well, boys, ready to milk?" she asked seriously.

"We did!" we exclaimed with pride.

"Ah, I have good helpers!" she said. At supper she told Pa that we were good milkers.

Our pa was always planning to break more sod, and he did through much work and grief of various kinds. He and Uncle Charlie had two walking plows to begin with, but Pa kept talking of getting a sulky plow. This year he did. The plow needed four or six horses to pull it, but it went faster and the farmer could ride now rather than walk as he had done for years, guiding the single beam by hand.

The new plow broke up more land for us boys to drag down, walking behind a one-section drag and old Fanny. Sometimes, we'd sneak a ride, sitting astride her harness and holding onto a hame, the wood part that sticks up from the collar. If Pa caught us he'd scold us, "She got enough to do without you ride yet! You get down and walk." Well, we had gotten a little rest anyway, and we were learning to take care of our working stock.

Pa had his hands full with trying to carve a profitable farming operation out on the gumbo soil and high hills. The first years we had good yields of grain, oats for milk cows, barley for hogs, and maybe some grain hay to sell or trade. Corn and the garden crops didn't do as well as they had in Minnesota and Iowa. The short season varieties hadn't been developed, and the short dry season of northern South Dakota wasn't the best for such crops.

It seems that there was much rain that summer, and just at the Fourth of July when there was to be a big celebration in Lemmon, the Grand River was flooding. We didn't go, supposing the celebration had been called off. Later we learned that it had been held and we had missed it.

"I don't think I can stand it," I said one morning while Chris and I were watering hogs.

My brother looked surprised. "Stand what? The sun? Ma's breakfast?" he teased.

"School!" I grumbled. "That old arithmetic and ..."

"We know our tables now, we even got a new school house! It'll be all right, wait and see," Chris promised.

I would have been happy to wait a year or two, but in a week we were hiking west over the prairie, lunch pails and books in hand. It was good to see our friends again, and the new school was nice. Our teacher was a reasonable woman, and things went well.

The sod schoolhouse in the spring of 1908. Marie Hamlin, Ester Priebe, Lyle Norton, Frances Snodgrass (teacher), Henry Miller, Frank Norton, Christoff Miller, Johnny Dunn, and Dave Hamlin.

Inside the building, we sat at double desks. There was a teacher's desk, chair, and a bench for classes in the front of the room. A round jacketless stove sat in about the middle of the room and nearly roasted us on one side while our other side shivered in cold weather. The stove pipe ran right up through the roof to become the chimney. We had no pictures unless someone brought one from a paper or magazine at home, no piano or record player, no playground equipment. It wouldn't be long before we had a bat and ball, as baseball was a big thing then. Lunch pails sat on the floor until noon when each student sat at his own desk to eat. The walls may have been papered with newspapers later, but I think not the first year.

After a while, the sod walls began to bulge here or there and someone would cover the bulge with a piece of lumber and prop it up with a branch or a pole. The school became the social center of the community. There were sometimes Friday night dances there and Saturday night card parties. I remember seeing a bunch of little tots covered with coats and sleeping on blankets on the floor while the music and dancing went on only feet from them. Mothers brought coffee and cake, and probably sandwiches for lunch. These were happy times, especially for the women who seldom went out.

It was the fall of 1908 that Pa came in late from the field. Mother and we boys were just finishing with the milking. "There's a dead cow over the hills," Pa said. "I want to get the hide before it's too late. Can you get along if I take the boys?"

Mother brought the lantern and Pa's skinning knife while she sent us for jackets. "It'll be cool before you get back," she said. So the cow died, I thought. The children had told us when we came from school how Pa had clapped a saddle onto the nearest horse and without even properly fastening the girths, had ridden furiously after the cows that had gotten into the corn field. At least one had eaten too much green corn, and now she was dead.

Over the hills west, we followed a trail for a while. Then it seemed we were driving into the dark, shadowy hills themselves. Prince snorted low and suddenly before I saw the poor cow lying on her side with legs sticking straight out. Pa pulled the team to a stop and we all got out of the wagon.

Pa lit the lantern. This was about the size and shape of the gas lanterns some use for camping and winter fishing, but it burned kerosene and offered a poor light and a lot of oily smell. Pa handed the lantern to me by its long wire loop handle, then he began drawing the knife over the whetstone. Back and forth, until we wondered if he would ever be ready.

"Now I'll just slit this down here," Pa said. "Christoff, you hold this tight for me. Henry, hold the lantern so the light is where we are working."

That sounded like the work of a few minutes. We hoped so, but things don't go that fast. The horses snorted again, and Chris and I jumped. "What's a matter you guys?" Pa chuckled.

"They won't leave us. Quiet, you sons-a-guns," he growled at the horses. "Tomorrow, you go to town."

The talk eased my fears a little, but then a coyote howled. When that happens, a whole chorus joins in from three or four directions. I crowded closer with the lantern, sure we were completely surrounded by the wild dogs. They'd been eyeing that cow all afternoon from the hill-top dens, and waiting for darkness and the feast.

"Take it easy!" Pa grumbled. "The coyotes are close to half a mile away. Watch what you're doing here. You'll have Chris losing a thumb," he warned. "Keep the light where it'll do us some good!" Finally the cow was half skinned and Pa and Chris rolled it over downhill. The blame coyotes cut loose again! Shivers ran up and down my spine.

I didn't even have the courage to peek over my shoulder! The hill coyotes had called up some from along the river, and there were some way over north answering the barking and howling. One beast would yap, and then another. The howling and yelping echoed and re-echoed across the silent hills. It made goose flesh spring out all over a fellow! Bolder animals came near enough so we could hear then moving around in the grass. "Isn't that musical?" Pa chuckled as the yip-yapping went on.

His attempt to cheer us wasn't of much help. At long last the skin was hung over the side of the wagon box and we hastily clambered up. Pa turned the team toward home and blew out the light. The coyotes seemed to be howling right under the wagon.

Pa cursed, "All right, you dogs, she's yours. The hide should get shoes for the whole family, but it won't. Be lucky if I can get two pairs for a trade. What's that compared to losing a cow, and her calf too come spring?" He bit down hard on his pipe and slapped the team into a trot.

Later when we had gone to bed, Chris asked, "When were you the scaredest?"

"I don't know when else you mean, but I sure was scared!" I confessed remembering the howling.

"The time the bull put his head under the wagon box and lifted it up," Christoff reminded me.

I thought back to the day in Minnesota. We had been helping Pa throw off some hay when the bull had lifted the wagon box with his head, all the while bellowing loudly. Pa had taken a pitch fork and jabbed the animal until he had left us alone.

I can still see the big head and short stubby horns so near. The bull always bellowed and raged along the fence if he saw Mother in the yard. We guessed he didn't like her long, flowing skirts. She was bound to empty stove ashes near the watering tank and that never failed to bring the bull to paw at the ashes. Fortunately, Pa got rid of him before he hurt anyone.

"I guess I was most afraid tonight," I decided, "Pa made the bull go away."

The next time we walked to school, we cast many a glance in the direction of the coyote hills, believe me. But everything was the same as ever in daytime.

In very late summer or early fall of 1908 we heard the folks talk of "if" and "when" and "it." Something was being priced, ordered and paid for.

But children didn't ask questions so we waited. One day we came from school to find Pa and Uncle Charlie busily digging a large square hole in the yard. Hilda and Louie stood watching the shovels full of earth sail upward.

"What they doing?" I asked.

"Digging," Hilda told me, tossing her curls.

"What for?" Chris asked.

"For a hole," came Uncle Charlie's cheerful voice from below. Dirt stopped coming up. "Come and have look," we were invited.

"A new storm cellar?" I guessed.

Pa climbed out of the hole and leaned on his spade. "We are going to build a frame house right here, and this is the cellar," he said. Our pa was so pleased and proud that we felt good, too.

"When?" and "How?" we wanted to know.

"Just as soon as everyone's harvest is in. The fellows around will help and we'll pour a little foundation and get started. Now get going, there's cows to milk tonight, too."

The chosen spot was measured, trenches dug, and the cement poured. Pa and Uncle Charlie worked on the house when they had time. Many of the bachelors around the neighborhood came and helped. Most of them were glad to come for the chance to eat a woman's cooking and to visit with their friends.

There was Jim Keller who lived a couple miles north and would one day be our teacher; Myron Delap, who later moved to Mobridge and set up a soft drink business, and Mr. Carlson, who lived a mile south of us. Some days we could see quite a lot of progress, and other times no one had worked or it was the kind that doesn't show.

Along with building a house, Pa got involved in the political future of Perkins County. He had great hopes and dreams for the area. Late in the fall, Pa and Uncle Charlie sat smoking their pipes after supper. They had picked corn and it was comfortable to rest while the household sounds floated around them.

"Why Bison?" Uncle Charlie suddenly asked.

"Well, it's nearest the center of the county," Pa replied. We kept our eyes in the direction of the school books spread on one end of the table, but our ears and minds were on the discussion. Mother was washing dishes, her dishpan set on the back of the kitchen stove. Hilda carefully wiped all but the few pieces too large or fragile for five-year-old hands.

"Could as well a left it all in Corson County," our uncle said.

"It's got to be different, 'cause the east part is still Indian land, don't you see!" Pa fumed. "It should be called Perkins County after Judge Perkins. He's done a lot for the country."

"But Bison's not even on the rail line," Uncle Charlie pointed out.

"It will be. The stage ran past there from Bismarck to Deadwood, and the freighters run that way right along. They ain't gonna drive ox and mule teams there forever when they can build a railroad. Both Lemmon and Bison are right on the route," Pa concluded, sounding as if that settled it all.

We forgot to pretend we were studying and frankly stared at what our uncle said next. "Now with cars in the country, there'll be better roads and trucks coming. Already some are talking of hauling mail south. They might even take people like the trains do. And never need the rails to Bison," he predicted.

Pa held his pipe in his hand, tipped his chair back, and hooted with laughter! He slapped his knee and roared, "Why, them cars is a joke! They won't last two years in Dakota." And then he went on, "Without the railroad, the whole country'd die."

Uncle Charlie shook his head. "Not anymore, maybe once, but not now," he said evenly and quietly, like Grandpa Lang. "Now tell me why then, after the whole town of Seim moved to Lemmon to get to the rails, why should the county seat be way off down there?"

"The 'lection will tell," Pa said stubbornly. "Folks down south will vote for Bison. What you guys staring at?" he growled at us. "You ain't gonna learn much just lookin'!" The discussion ended. We had learned a lot.

By early winter, Pa had brought a new or used coal heating stove from Lemmon and installed it in the living room of the new house. Now painting and papering could be done. Mother made hundreds of trips from one house to the other as she answered questions, cooked meals for men, looked after her little folks, and helped anywhere she could.

The house was sixteen by thirty-two feet. The living room was on the north with a window in each outer wall. The center room served as kitchen and dining room and a small bedroom on the south completed the house. It was as good or big as most, and was better than many. One chilly sunny Saturday just before Christmas, the fire in the cook stove in the soddy was let die out after breakfast. As soon as chores were done, the little folks and all began the job of moving from one house to the other.

We carried small things by hand and Pa hitched Buck to the stoneboat to haul the cook stove and the heavy chest of drawers. Uncle Charlie was on hand to help.

After a long busy day, we celebrated by having a good hot supper cooked in the new house. This may well have been a little late after a stove pipe cutting session and some harsh language on Pa's part. Stove pipes always give more than their share of trouble.

Pa had told the neighbors that if the house was finished in time, we would host a neighborhood New Year's Eve dance. Now word went out that the house was finished, we were in, and the dance was upcoming.

As it happened, the evening was warm and there was very little snow. People came from far and wide in wagons and buggies. If it is cold and windy a wagon offers better protection. Hay or straw is put in the bottom and passengers ride down low protected by the wagon sides. If there is lots of snow a bobsled is used. A few may have had covered buggies, but not many.

This time, the family of my closest friend, Dave Hamlin, was late and people were beginning to ask and wonder. Perhaps someone was ill or the Hamlins were in trouble. I wandered to the window often and listened as best I could over the hubbub for any sound from the outside. Mr. Goedert, who lived west a few miles and whose name was said "Gator" was tuning up his fiddle for the evening's music.

Some of the fellows were picking up the tunes on mouth organs or harmonicas. I could see people beginning to worry. A shout of laughter rose from the older boys and young men standing around outside. We rushed to doors and windows to see what was causing the excitement. Coming slowly - as slowly as a horse can walk and two boys can trot - came the Hamlin buggy. The old riding pony was pulling, and holding up the other end of the neck yoke were my friend Dave and his brother. (The neck yoke is a round wooden rod which is fastened by straps to the horses' collars and holds up the end of the buggy pole or tongue. The boys held up the missing horse's end of the rod while the pony did the actual pulling.)

Mr. Hamlin led the pony, Mrs. Hamlin and the baby rode in the buggy, and other children walked or trotted beside the buggy.

"What happened?" "Lose a horse?" "Boys been naughty?" were some of the comments directed toward our laughing friends as they neared the buildings.

As the story unfolded, we learned that the Hamlin horses were running in the hills and fields as did many during the winter. There was only the pony at home and rather than miss the dance, the boys and their family improvised a method of travel. After dancing and games until midnight and lunch and visiting into the wee hours, they expected to make the same trip home. I'm quite sure we loaned them a horse to get home a little faster.

The story was to be told again and again and chuckled over and enjoyed for many years. Our house warming and the New Year's celebration of 1908-into-1909 has been a happy memory for me.

-8-

YEAR OF SURPRISES, 1909

The first surprise came soon after the New Year when we were told that there would be no school that winter. Whether our teacher had married, moved, or just quit, I don't know but we had no school. The new sod building stood silent and empty except for the once-a-month times when the neighbors gathered for dances. The first ones there would build up a fire with wood brought from home, then dusted the desks and benches. Others brought more wood as well as lunch, and the parties would go on until the wood was gone and the building began to grow cold.

Children's books were taken home with the idea that we would do some school work. We probably did much less than our parents intended. At different times, Uncle Charlie coached us at reading or numbers before he would take us trapping, rabbit hunting, or show us some of his tricks.

We trapped the same ponds as we had the winter before. We hunted jackrabbits often, since they were one of the few sources of meat in the early years of homesteaders. Everyone ate rabbit up until about 1917 when the rabbits became diseased.

Pa or Uncle Charlie or both of them taught us to play checkers, and we played quite a lot. We were introduced to some card games, and Uncle Charlie and we boys revived the game of "Jack and Jill." It didn't take us long to figure out that our uncle was simply putting a different finger on the table when his bits of paper were "gone." We had lots of fun with Hilda and Louie and the game.

"Is your hand as tough as mine?" our uncle asked one day. We hoped so, but guessed not or some such boyish thing. Uncle Charlie took Mother's tea kettle from the stove and set it on his big palm. The four of us gasped and Mother just shook her head. The next second, Uncle Charlie grabbed that pot and set it back on the stove! "As soon as it stops boiling, it gets hotter," he explained. "They say the boiling brings cooler air into the water."

"Ach!" Mother scoffed. "Anyone knows if it boils it's hotter than when it doesn't."

Uncle Charlie laughed. "You want to try it?"

"Nein!" Mother said, "And I don't want anyone else trying it either." She looked hard at her children.

Once we heard a strange swishing noise in the kitchen. The noise went along with comments like, "Oops, look out! There it goes!" In a moment we youngsters were all standing in the doorway gawking into the kitchen. This was what the men hoped for.

There was Uncle Charlie holding Mother's big enamel dishpan in both hands and swaying back and forth as he moved the pan in a small circle. The noise came from inside the pan. Our uncle stopped the movement and there was a rattling sound as something fell and rolled in the pan. "Anybody want to try that?" he asked.

"Yah," we chorused, all stepping closer.

"Let Hank try first," our uncle said. He handed me the dishpan and I could see a silver dollar lying in the bottom. Uncle Charlie stood behind me and turned our backs to any windows. Then he took hold of the pan beside my hands. "We'll just spin slow and easy now, and watch the dollar," he said. We began spinning the dishpan.

"Easy now," Mother cautioned, "I don't want that flying in anybody's face." The dollar slid up and around and around near the top of the pan. I was beside myself with pleasure as we spun the pan together and the dollar swished by me. Then Uncle Charlie let go and left me on my own. It wasn't a couple seconds before the pesky dollar flew out onto the floor.

"You work too hard at it, boy," Pa said. Uncle Charlie motioned for Chris to come and try. "Now just spin it easy," he repeated. "Just enough to keep the dollar going." I've done this with a fifty cent piece now that silver dollars are hard to come by. Hold the hands across from each other and keep the motion smooth and just strong enough to keep the coin going. They will fly out if you go too fast or get careless. With a little practice, almost anyone can do this stunt. We thought it a great pastime.

We rode along when Pa and Uncle Charlie took a team and stoneboat to the creek for water. In cold weather, this was done every other day or so. Pa cussed as he chopped the thick ice with an ax so the cattle could drink. Then while the stock took turns at the hole in the ice, we hauled up pail after pail of water from the well and poured it into the barrel to be hauled to the house. "Now don't get yourself wet," we were warned. But a boy can handle only so many pails of water before he gets splashed. We got home with stiff, frozen jeans more than once.

One time, Uncle Charlie went a little way away from the rest of us and began to swing his pail of water higher and higher. I wondered just what he had in mind. Our uncle suddenly swung the water pail completely over his head! The nearly full pail came down in a neat arc without spilling a bit. We broke into big grins. "Ya dang fool!" our pa hollered. "What ya show them that for! Now they'll try it and get wet!"

Our Uncle Charlie chuckled and said, "Don't try that until it's warmer or your pa'll lick us all three." We laughed at the vision of Pa lickin' our uncle. Charlie was a head taller than Pa. The next time we boys and Uncle Charlie hauled water, we begged to try the stunt. Our uncle shook his head, "Not here, if you got wet you'd catch a cold. Maybe back at the place."

When the water was safely delivered to the house, Uncle Charlie handed us each a half-full pail of water. "That's my drinking water," he said with a grin. "Don't spill it." We followed him a little way from the house. "Now keep your arm straight and swing from the shoulder. Let your shoulder and wrist do the turning." He demonstrated the swing. "Begin at the bottom and don't stop when you get to the top." We were afraid we'd get wet, so we made big hard swings, but before long we could swing the pails without any trouble.

"What keeps the water in?" Chris needed to know.

"You're going fast," Uncle Charlie explained. "The water tries to swing farther than the pail, so it stays in the bottom." There are modern words for that, but he was right. When we were older, we tried swinging pails of milk. We had to try it with eggs as well!

Early in the New Year the voters - men only - gathered at the local polling place and made their wishes known concerning the county seat of government. Pa spent the day at the school helping to clerk the election, and late that night he and a neighbor made the trip to town with the ballot box.

The election "told", just as Pa had predicted. Bison won by something like fifteen votes and became the new county seat of Perkins County. It is yet today, and no rail line has ever been built there.

Lumber and other building needs were hauled to Bison from the railroad at Lemmon in hopes that building would begin as soon as the weather warmed up. Later when the courthouse was ready, the county records were moved to Bison by ox teams and many wagons. These oxen came to my mind years later when I found the crescent shaped shoe of an ox along their route when I worked on a road building crew. I treasured the shoe for many years. I liked to think it was from one of the "county" oxen.

By early March, we were bored with staying at home and tired of winter. Life seemed to be an endless round of cold dark mornings, chores, wood cutting, checkers, little school work, more chores and long evenings. Trapping was over and even checkers wasn't much fun. One day Pa and Uncle Charlie went into town. We were at supper when we heard the sounds of the team and bobsled on the hard snow in the yard.

Chris and I grabbed caps and jackets to be ready to help unload whatever had been brought home. The sled stood in front of the door, and the men handed out boxes and bags.

Quite a stack of goods had been set inside the house and I turned to take the next object when Pa handed me a furry, round puppy about two months old.

We "oh-ed" and "ah-ed" and fussed over the puppy. Chris reached over to pat it and Louie and Hilda begged us to bring it over so they could see and pet it from inside the door. "Whose is it?" Chris asked.

"For Mamas," Pa said. "She like a dog and miss Jack."

Tears stood in Mother's eyes. "For us all," she said. "Come, bring him just a minute, then he goes to the barn." So our new dog was brought into the house for all to admire. When we returned from putting the pup safely in the barn, Mother was telling the younger children about Jack. "... about this tall and dark and shaggy, but gentle, and he watched after the boys when they were little," she said. "When the grass was tall around the yard, I just called Jack, then I knew the boys would be where he came from. Many let stock run loose like here and Jack kept the cows away from the house and my gardens."

Mother chuckled. "You boys remember the fat salesman?" she asked. We nodded, grinning. The big, dressy fellow had come while Mother was in the garden. "Good morning, Ma'am," he began. "I have everything you need, dusts and ..." He might have gone on and on, but Mother had snapped her fingers for Jack who lay nearby in the shade. The big dog appeared at her side about the time the man turned from climbing out of his buggy. "Now," he puffed. "Ah, what a nice dog! Does he bite?" He took a step closer.

Mother's temper rose quickly. "Oh, you're going to try him?" she snapped. Jack growled softly and moved forward a step. The fat man all but fell into his buggy in his haste to be gone. We had watched from the porch.

"Another man came to the door to try to sell me something I didn't need," Mother went on. "I saw him come to the house, so I called Jack and he stood by me at the door. The man say, 'Now that's a nice dog, does he bite?' And I say, 'You want that I should try him?' The fellow turn white and hurry to his buggy. A woman alone a lot needs a dog like that. Here we have no salesmen, but we need a dog to bark if a snake comes in the yard."

"Remember the dog that ran past the place in Minnesota?" Pa asked now. Both Mother and Uncle Charlie nodded. "A strange dog ran by close to the farm, all foamy around the face and just running away like crazy," Pa told us. "The funny thing is, Jack'd always run off any stray dog. But this time he hid under the porch. Never could figure it out, but that dog was sick and Jack knew it. The dog didn't hurt a thing, just ran past." I barely recall the incident but in later years, I've decided the dog might have had rabies and Jack sensed it. We didn't hear of rabies until later, but it's likely.

At last the snow melted, the river broke up, and the meadowlarks returned. The larks were welcome signs of spring, especially since there are few birds in the prairie areas. We saw crows, prairie chickens, perhaps magpies, and in summer, the larks. Men went to work in the fields and boys herded cattle day after day. One morning we boys sat on Brownie as our uncle opened the gates to let out the stock. "You'll have to teach your pup to be a cattle dog now," Uncle Charlie told us. "Maybe he'll get as good as the dogs at a place where I worked once."

"What did they do?" we wanted to know.

"They chased cattle, boy did they chase cattle!"

"Tell us, you want to anyway," Chris teased.

"The boss left one day, and while he was gone the cows got out. So I set the dogs on them to get them in where they belonged. There were two big dogs, and they ran the stock in and out of the corral before I got the gate shut. Then the dogs and the dang cattle ran all over the farm yard, and up and back around the place. I hollered and whistled and cussed those fool dogs. But they wouldn't quit!" Uncle Charlie explained.

We laughed, picturing our uncle helplessly calling the runaway dogs. "Pretty quick, the whole caboodle of them ran through the old lady's garden," our uncle went on. "That was too much! She came out of the house stomping and storming and yelled, 'Whoa!' Why, those dogs just slid on their heels, they stopped so fast! Then she cussed them in Russian."

"Are you sure it was the dogs she was cussing?" I teased, kicking Brownie away so fast we almost spilled my surprised brother from behind the saddle.

Our pa hired a man with a horse-powered well rig to bore a well on the farm. The drill was something like a large, cogged wheel mounted horizontally on a heavy wagon frame. Two big horses walked around and around to bore the hole in the ground. The job took a couple days or more and the horses were kept and fed in our barn. Late one evening, I realized that I had forgotten to feed those horses. Being a normal scared-of-the-dark kid, I said nothing. But fathers have a way of checking up on things, and before long I was asked if I had fed the man's horses.

Our pa rarely laid a hand on us, but he had a hard, cold look that could "just about put a boy through the floor" and we didn't lie to him. So I confessed that I had forgotten. "So go feed them," he said. I stumbled across the dark yard as the flickering light of the kerosene lantern cast spooky, long shadows. I reached the black interior of the barn to feed two strange horses, then got myself back to the house and into bed. I died about a thousand deaths out there, but I remembered to take care of stock before dark after that.

The well was finished and a pump mounted at the top. What a treat to have water so handy! Right in the yard, mind you. "Maybe next year we can get a windmill," Pa half promised.

Now with a better plow, we had some fifty acres under cultivation. Still, oats and barley were the main crops. These would be cut as hay and fed, straw and all, to hogs and milk cows. Corn was picked for hogs and the stalks cut and tied in a bundle with a stalk for twine. This was called fodder and wasn't silage by any means, but it was feed for milk cows. Potatoes were planted along the side or at the end of the corn field. There was no sweet corn; we ate field corn before it got too hard.

The garden may well have been enlarged to match our appetites and abilities. It was wise to plant in a low spot as there might be more moisture there.

The garden patch was plowed in the spring with a team and walking plow the first years and later done with the sulky plow. This plow made only one fourteen- or sixteen-inch furrow so a field took a long time. The garden went quickly once Pa got to it.

We dragged down the plowing with the one section drag or harrow to break up the lumps and smooth the rough spots. Then Mother and Hilda, in long skirts, (women didn't have slacks then) went out with hoes and rakes and worked the ground some more. Sometimes one of us boys had to help them.

My parents had rules for which things should be planted at different stages of the moon. I believe if a root is the food, we planted at the dark of the moon; if we ate that which grows above the ground, the crop was planted at full moon. I do not think there are scientific basis for the rules, but older people went by them and they had good gardens. Potatoes were supposed to be planted on Good Friday, but many years this is just too early.

Picking rocks off fields is supposed to be easy for young backs and arms. Let me tell you, it isn't! After a couple of hours, every stone is bigger and heavier than the last one and your feet really get to dragging. In our area much of the soil is yellow clay called gumbo, and if it is even a little damp, it sticks to the feet of men and horses in great balls, and gums up wagon and machine wheels making work impossible. Water doesn't soak in easily, and the surface gets slick and "greasy" after just a light shower. This made farming and traveling very difficult and was a sad change from the rich soils of Minnesota and Iowa. Most of such land is in permanent pasture again. It should never have been plowed in the first place but no one knew that until it was done.

After a rain, when it was too wet for haying or field work, we found ourselves mending or setting out new fence. Fencing itself is a rather pleasant job on a cool, sunny morning with the meadowlarks singing. But it seemed that we were always plagued by thousands of mosquitoes. We boys would be continually swatting, slapping and scratching. "What's a matta, you guys?" Pa would demand gruffly.

"The mosquitoes," we'd grumble, continuing to work with one hand and swat with the other.

"Aw, mosquitoes!" he'd say. "Look, not a one here."

To our astonishment they weren't bothering him, but the insects swarmed around us boys. It was several years before someone observed that "Pa's pipe is so strong that the mosquitoes don't hang around him."

One day at breakfast, Mother would tell us boys she wanted all the crocks of old grease from the cellar and plenty of wood before we went about our day's work. This meant soap making. Mother mixed boughten lye with the bacon and other frying greases she had saved. She cooked it together into a soft jelly-like mass. Then she poured the strong smelling mixture into large flat pans. When the soap was cooled and not yet hard, Mother cut it into bars with a sharp knife. This was our supply of soap for hands, baths, shampooing, dishes, and laundry until it was gone when Mother would make soap again.

The wild fruits ripened in late summer and Mother would walk to a patch of plum or chokecherry trees, pick a big sack of fruit, and carry it home. Sometimes she had help, but many times she did this herself.

The fruits were cooked, the juice poured off and strained through a clean cloth to take out stems, pits and pulp. The clear juice was carefully measured and sugar added in exact ration. The juice and sugar were cooked together until it was just right.

Mother would stick a fork into her boiling jelly, and if the spaces between the tines became coated when she lifted the tool, the jelly was done. The ladies made it a point to get some rather green fruits into the jelly pot, as these had the pectin necessary to get the jelly to jell. The white foam was skimmed from the jelly and the hot syrupy jelly was carefully poured into scalded jars, covered with melted wax and set to cool. The jelly would be carried to the cellar and stored for winter time use on bread and pancakes. Sometimes the jelly remained like syrup, then we used it just as we used regular syrup. Mother also made plum butter. The pulp of the plums was mashed and pits removed, then Mother cooked the fruit with sugar and spices. The plum butter was much like apple butter, only a bit more tart.

One time Uncle Charlie took Chris and me to a circus. It may have been this summer. The old papers say a circus played in Lemmon that year. I saw a clown with a baby pig. The pig was dressed up in a bonnet. The clown carried the piglet under his arm and let it suck on a baby bottle. Then he would have a quick drink on it himself, or make it appear that he did. The pig would squeal and make a fuss, and the clown would give her another drink. This was almost too much for me!

We looked forward to school and to seeing our friends, although now we had picnics and ball games where we saw the other boys during the summer. Also the herd boys often rode and worked and played together. Hilda began school in 1909, so we had the responsibility of looking after her. Hilda was an easy girl to get along with so we didn't mind.

As we walked from school in late September, I thought I heard a rooster crow. But we didn't have any chickens at home!

I glanced at Chris and Hilda. We all looked at each other and then toward the farm yard. Farther north, we could see the team and wagon coming from the direction of Lemmon. We hurried, hoping to get home about the time Pa did. We could hear him singing in German as the wagon came nearer.

Mother and Louie came to the door on hearing our shouts, and we all met Pa as he came around the house. Our mother shielded her eyes from the sun with her hand and called up, "Been to a sale?" She stepped around to the back of the wagon. "The dresser from home! Papa sent it."

Our pa nodded, "They said at the store there was some stuff from Minnesota." He set a crate containing a young rooster and nine hens out on the ground.

"We got to get a corner fixed up for these birds in the barn," he stated. We moved out of the way as the wagon was backed nearer the door of the house. "Nice of him to send it," Pa remarked as he began unloading the heavy dresser. "Help here now, boys don't let Mamas do it. Don't know why he sent this," Pa pretended to be grumpy as he set a rocking cradle out of the wagon.

"Oh, is das recht?" (That right) Mother smiled.

Christoff untied the rope around the dresser, and I pulled open the first drawer. Grandma had sent garden seed contained inside canning jars which protected the seed from mice in the baggage car. She knew that if we'd had any garden at all, Mother would have saved seed, so she sent some kinds you can't save in the north, like beets and carrots, maybe some lettuce, too. There may have been melon and pumpkin seeds and perhaps peas and beans, as well.

The bottom drawer seemed to hold only an old cloth. We pulled it out and discovered a new pieced quilt. Mother handed Chris the note to read. "Happy Birthday, Carrie" in our Aunt Mary's handwriting. Mother wept, but soon regained her composure. On shaking out the quilt we found new knit mittens for four children. Bless dear Grandma! Last spring we had worn mitts made of the good parts of worn out overalls over our other worn mittens. With the "pants" mitts over these we would be snug.

"Nothing for me?" Pa teased.

Mother sniffed. "You get the cradle," she retorted.

One day the end of October, we came from school to find that cradle occupied by new baby brother, Billy, the first of the family to be born on the homestead.

-9-
ONE MORE YEAR, 1910

Pa and Uncle Charlie hauled lumber and cut poles from trees for the short wooden windmill tower. They planned and measured and began building. The mill head was installed at the top and the pump rod strung from the pump to the gears above. The everlasting wind turned the big wheel, which ran the gears and pulled the pump rod up and down to pump water. What fun to let the wind do the hard work of pumping! Only once in a while we would have to fasten up the handle and pump a bit of water. The well and windmill were certainly a step forward for the farm and made life much easier for all of us. Mother was happy that the water was soft, non-mineral. That is the kind that women like best for washing clothes and children.

We were proud that the farm would be ours in another year. This spring we boys, near ten and eleven, were considered big enough to stay out of school and help with the farming. One of us would stay home a day and do the dragging, and after school the other would come and take over. This wasn't the end of the day. It was milking time and we brought the cows on our way from the fields.

Ours weren't the big high-producing Holsteins that most dairymen milk now. They were smaller cows, mostly red or roan. A good cow gave four gallons of milk a day, not five or more each milking. Some gave only a gallon a milking. Cows got little grain and no good alfalfa hay like now.

It is of interest to me that the gentleman who introduced alfalfa to much of South Dakota later became my boss in Day County. The late Henry Hansmeier, I understand, began working with hardy alfalfa in about 1912. Some in the Lemmon area were trying to grow alfalfa by the early 1920s.

Milking time was Mother's time with her boys. She told us her family history and other things we needed to know. Mother told stories of her childhood in Iowa and about her family. She told how her dad, our Grandpa Lang, had come to America in about 1865 when he was a teenager. The great Chicago fire was in 1871, and Grandpa was on his way home from work on an underground railway. The trains stopped to let off anyone who would stay and fight fires.

Our grandparents Lang had been married in Chicago, and when Mother and Aunt Anna were little girls they had moved to Iowa. The children had gone to a United Brethren church school for a couple of years where they spoke and wrote German. The boys of the family had gone on to another school.

There were Aunt Anna, Mother, our dear Uncle Charlie, Uncle John and little sisters, Mary and Tina, only a bit older than Chris and me. They seemed more like friends than aunts to us. Mother's family is all gone: Aunt Anna Lang Graffinteen is buried near Pipestone, Minnesota, and Uncle Charlie Lang at Sanborn, North Dakota. Aunt Mary Reedy lived in California for some years before her death shortly after Mother's. Aunt Tina married and homesteaded in Canada where I presume she is buried, Uncle John Lang is gone, but I cannot say where he lived. There is some family in Iowa.

Our mother would never allow us to tickle each other or the smaller children. She told of a lad whose older brothers had tickled him until he became ill. They called the condition "goosy." We would call it nerves. "So we will have no tickling here. I don't want anyone getting goosy," Mother warned.

We certainly did more work than children of this day, but I doubt if we had more to do than most of our friends did. In a large family without water in the house and other conveniences, there was a lot that needed doing. As I said, Mother was a small person. Maybe her size made her seem busier, but she was always rushing about. Mother carried water or saw to it that an older child did it. She baked bread for an ever-increasing number of appetites, and she washed clothes on a wash board for years.

Our mother sewed and mended in the evenings. She made socks and mittens from old clothing, using a garment for a pattern. Winter evenings, Mother made quilts and rugs. Summers, she worked outside and often did her baking and house cleaning into the early morning. Mother milked cows and raised a garden in heat, drought, and sometimes hordes of grasshoppers. Many times our little mother helped with grain shocking or shoveling, even if she wouldn't have to. Mother liked the outdoors and let Hilda take over in the house as soon as she could handle the work. Hilda was a tall girl and I expect that she did a grownup's work at quite an early age.

Add to Mother's interests and activities a baby every year or two. We all got experience at looking after the little ones. As each one grew, he was given his share of chores to do. The smaller children helped look after chickens and geese, picked up wood and cobs for stove fuel. They helped with weeding in the garden and picked vegetables, and ran errands for everyone. Little sisters learned which is the business end of a needle by sewing long strips of rags together and rolling them into a ball for Mother to use in her braided rugs. There was always cleaning, mending, and dishes to do, as well as helping "Mamas" with the next babe.

Usually Mother managed not to keep the little folks at a job when they were tired; she was good that way. But jobs that older children helped with had to be finished. You don't milk half the cow, then go to school no matter how late you are. And you chopped tomorrow's wood in moonlight if need be.

The churn was a stone crock holding about two gallons. To make butter, fill the crock about half full of cream, then put in the dasher, a stick like a broom handle with a cross or "X" of wood at the bottom. Put the lid on with the stick coming up through the center hole. Now you churn by lifting and lowering the dasher until the cream turns to butter. This can take from fifteen minutes to two hours depending on the age, temperature, and richness of the cream. We got very tired and bored with the job, believe me. Mother would have one start the churning and after while another child would take over and so on.

Mother could hear the churn from anywhere in the house. Sometimes she would call "I don't hear much churning going on in there." Finally we heard the splashy sound that meant chunks of butter were floating in buttermilk. Someone older dipped out the butter into a large pan and poured the buttermilk into a crock or jar to be stored in a cool place. Buttermilk is a good drink and very good for making pancakes. The butter was put back into the churn to be washed.

Someone carried a pail of fresh, cold well water and poured part of it into the churn. Mother replaced the cover and dasher and washed the butter in the churn. This water was poured off and the process repeated two or three times. The rinsing water was saved for pigs. Now Mother worked the butter. She salted it in the large bowl, and with a wooden butter paddle pressed the water from the butter. Butter will not keep well if it contains water, so Mother was extra careful with the butter she would take to town for trading. Mother tasted the butter and added more salt if it was needed, then she pressed it into a loaf pan and cut it into blocks. The blocks were carefully wrapped and stored in the storm cellar. In the summertime the butter was yellow because the cows were eating grass, but butter always came out white in the winter.

This year, 1910 was a good year. The crops looked so beautiful that our pa and uncle invested in more machinery. A grain binder was bought to serve on both farms.

It was a thrill to us boys, and I think to the men too, to see the machine brought into the yard. Even better was watching the wooden slats of the reel draw the tall yellow stalks of grain down onto the sickle as the binder moved across the field a few weeks later. A huge lugged drive wheel dug into the ground, and gears from it turned the reel, moved the canvas that carried the grain to the tie, turned the tying mechanism, and finally kicked out the finished bundles of grain. Four big horses were needed to power the machine.

Now it was time for the whole family to go out to the field and set ten or so heavy bundles into a shock, a teepee-shaped mound of grain. We were taught by our mother and uncle how to set the grain with the heads at the top to dry in the sun. If it should rain, the water would run away from the seeds and they wouldn't sprout. It's hard to tell anyone how to set a shock; you just watch, then try and eventually you can do it right. The grain shocks might have to stand for a month or more before the threshing rig came, so they had to be done right.

"Oops," Mother would say, "I think maybe the wind blow this one down." So we went back and labored over the bundles until our shock stood to Mother's approval. Harvest is during the hot part of the year and shocking was always hot, tiresome work. The long scratchy stubble makes walking hard, and the soil is often loose and dusty. But a field of shocked grain is a beautiful sight.

Before most folks had threshers, a few did custom threshing for a share of grain or at a flat rate. They had a machine called a fourteen horse thresher, or a twelve or a sixteen, depending on the size or the machine. The machine I saw was powered by fourteen horses moving in a large circle. The eveners for each team were hitched to spokes coming from a central hub. The horses turned the hub, which was fastened by gears to a long pole running horizontal to the ground, kind of a power-take-off. This power shaft, through more gears on the other end, ran the threshing rig. Even old experienced horses were skittish about stepping over the turning shaft at first, but soon they calmed down and stepped over it every time around.

The machine itself, or the one I remember, was mostly wood on the outside. The "innards" would have some iron. Once the horses had the thing running, the fellows who hauled bundles, shocks from the fields, would begin pitching them into the machine. With much grinding and clattering, the grain was knocked from the heads and straw. The straw was dumped out one way and the threshed grain run out past a sort of fan that blew away some of the chaff. The finished grain ran into bags below.

After harvest, came school. If we weren't through with fall work, Pa kept one of us home one day and the other the next. He said this way we'd both get some schooling. Christoff was good at math but he hated to read. I enjoyed the reading but never could like math. We helped each other in the evenings.

The English language, brought by us boys and Pa was spreading into the home. Mother asked about things in German and we answered in English. We turned more and more to English and in a few years German would be as strange to the little ones as English had once been to Chris and me.

Some of our school friends were Swedish and Norwegian children. As we all struggled to master English, we began to notice that they talked "funny." They noticed that about us, too! I suppose we hurt each other's feelings from time to time but mostly we learned together.

One day as we ate our cold lunches at school, Dave, one of our friends asked, "Do you know my dog's name, Miller?" No one did, but we guessed at several anyway. "You know," said Dave while his family smothered their giggles.

"No, I don't," I said. "What is it?"

"You know," he said again.

I was getting angry. "How would I know your fool dog's name?"

"It's 'You know,'" Dave said again. He explained that in the Norse languages a "J" is sounded like an English "Y". The dog's name was Juno, but the family called him You-know or Yuno. We shared the joke, and at supper we tried it on Pa. He reacted the same way I had, only sooner. We explained and Mother who had a great sense of humor smoothed things over.

"Yah," she sighed, "it is a hard thing to learn. One day I was in the meat market and a woman wanted some meat."

The story goes like this: The lady asked for "sheep" meat.

"I have no mutton," the butcher told her.

"I don't want mutton, I want 'sheep meat,'" the woman said.

"Mutton is sheep meat," the butcher pointed out.

The woman sighed. "It's for the threshers, and I don't have much money!" she explained.

"Then you don't want mutton?"

"No, I want some 'sheeper' meat."

The man helped her with her purchase and she went her way. Whether she knew or not, she had our mother's sympathy.

There was a Russian neighbor lady who would say, "Yes, yes, it's nobody's fault; just one of those blame things." But in her broken English, it came out, "Yup, yup, nopoddy's fault; chust one uh dose dom 'tings."

Our parents had some trouble with the English language as long as they lived. A chair became a "share"; Pa got his "cun" and went to shoot a skunk; we "wisited" the neighbors and "chust" had a "goot" time, especially if there was a bit of "vine".

Before it got too cold to work outside, our farm boasted a new frame barn. As with the house, different neighbors had helped with the construction. The two grain bins, alley way, and four horse stalls went up rapidly. One of our parents' dreams was a porch along the east side of the house. A floor was laid and posts set to hold up the roof. Soon a twelve-by-thirty-foot porch stretched the length of the house. A door was cut so that summer suppers could be taken from the warm kitchen and served out on that shady porch. This was quite a gift to Mother.

Maybe this was the first fall that we had enough eggs or maybe the first time our mother had the time, but she carefully pricked eggs at both ends and blew out the contents so she could save the shells. What a surprise to find the tree-limb Christmas tree trimmed with colored egg shells! Plums or choke-cherry juice would serve as red dye, onion skins would make yellow, blue water from new jeans might color something (even if you didn't want it colored!) Mother was very clever; she may have thought up ways to get other colors.

Again, we hosted the neighborhood New Year's Eve dance. It had been a prosperous year with rains and a good harvest. All who filed with us were looking forward to proving up and owning their farms in the spring. Christmas and New Year were joyous occasions.

-10-
PROVED UP, 1911

Since most winters are about the same as the last, this seems a good place to tell of the few diversions we enjoyed before spring work began.

Sometime during the school term there was a basket sale or a pie social. Each of the ladies from ten-year-old girls through the older grandmothers fixed a lunch for two in a box or basket and decorated the box as prettily as she could manage. One of our teachers fixed her box to look like a steamship, complete with smokestacks. It caused quite a stir. If the occasion was a pie social, a pie was baked by each lady of the household. These were wrapped and the package decorated.

Each mother took cups and forks for her family and a couple bought coffee pots filled with steaming brew. These coffee pots had large bottoms and tapered toward the top. They held as much as two and one-half gallons of coffee and were made of metal with an enamel coating. There was a looped handle at the top for carrying and a handle on the side for pouring. The pots would be wrapped in an old coat or blanket to hold the heat. Lemonade or milk may have been brought for the children some of the time.

After a short program, singing bee or spelling contest, a citizen would step forward, lift high the first basket or pie and ask, "What am I bid for this beautiful bit of cookery?" Children's baskets were most often kept separate and sold to the younger boys at smaller prices. Little girls' baskets might start at a dime, and be bid with much coaching from fathers, brothers, and the auctioneer, up to fifty cents. The youngster who had purchased it would unwrap the pie or box and on top find a slip of paper telling which girl had brought it. With much blushing, he would locate the little lady and sit with her while they shared lunch or pie.

Then the real fun began! The selling of the teen and older young folks' baskets came next. We knew quite well who was "sweet on" who around the neighborhood. If we knew that Jack was hoping to buy Mary's basket, some of the other guys would bid it up and really make him pay for it. Sometimes Jack couldn't meet the price and one of his chums would share the girl's lunch and her company.

Then it was Jack's turn to get even: he might step over to Jane's little brother and whisper, "Ten cents says you don't know which is Jane's box."

The dime shining in his palm was too much and before little brother remembers that Jane has promised him much harm if he tells, he indicates the basket and the dime is his. Jack buys Jane's box lunch and eats with his friend's girl. After this they may ride home together, all good friends.

Many times, the girls packed double boxes which were sold to two fellows. This proved more fun and less embarrassing for the younger folks.

Some married couples made it a point that Pa buy Ma's basket, while most bought and lunched as the selling went. The unmarried lads were embarrassed to have gotten a married lady's basket and be eating with her and her little children. Most everyone kept coming so the socials must have been successful.

Money from the sale of pies or lunches was used to buy things that the school needed, like maps, a record player or playground equipment.

How did we light the building for evening socials? We brought kerosene lamps from home until the school could buy one. In later years, some brought gas lanterns that gave a bright white light but had to have air pumped into the gas tank often.

The spring of 1911 was early, warm and dry.

The little snow melted and the dry grass was whipped by the winds. Early in March our pa made the two-day trip to Bison to apply for the title to our land. According to the Perkins County records he got the title on March third. Pa and Uncle Charlie left after chores one morning and expected to be home late in the afternoon the next day.

How well I remember starting home from school on that awful day! As soon as we turned north we saw a tower of smoke rising skyward in the direction of home. Chris handed me his lunch pail and books and he ran ahead to see if he could help. Hilda and I followed as fast as a little girl in a long skirt can travel.

Mother met us at the west edge of the yard. She had little Billy by the hand and a frightened Louie clung to her skirt. "The new barn is burning," she said sadly, though that was plain to see.

We shuddered as the terrible screams of trapped horses met our ears. We were upwind and out of the way of the neighbor men who were throwing pails full of water on the roof of the house. That roof was so hot it steamed when the water hit! "They couldn't get the little calves out, or the new team." Our tough little mother was trying hard not to cry. "All the harness left is on the ones Pa's driving."

The new young team, that Pa hadn't even used yet, finally stopped screaming. We stood in shocked silence as the barn burned to the ground. Neighbors had come when they saw smoke and had saved our home. One of those men came to tell Mother he thought it safe for us to go into the house. We went but wandered out again, and Mother didn't insist that we stay in. The men stood resting and talking as they watched lest the wind change and send sparks into hay stacks or onto the roof.

A team and buggy came tearing in from the north. Pa was home! Brokenly our mother told him the sad story while Uncle

Charlie and the other men stood at a respectful distance. I was surprised to see my pa near tears and I felt sorry for him. I picked up little Billy; Pa put an arm around our mother and a hand on Chris' shoulder. "You done all you could, no one could do more." He took a deep breath, "How did it start?"

"Little boys pick up matches you leave lying around," Mother said bitterly. "Lucky they didn't stay in there. They got scared and tried to cover the fire with hay ..." I hope the little boys weren't punished. I don't recall that they were. We had all had enough for one day. Ever after that our mother harped at Pa to keep his matches in his pockets. I can still hear the horses screaming and have always had a great fear of fire.

"This is the kind of things makes a man old," Pa muttered. We would hear this many times in the next few years. "And on the day I prove up. All this in five years!"

Before spring work Uncle Charlie made a trip to Minnesota by train. He returned with seed grain and a small gift for each of us. Big boys as we were, he got stuffed toys for us. Mine was a dog about eight inches high. Chris got a cat, and Hilda received a doll. I don't know what was brought for our parents or the little boys, but I treasured my dog for many years.

Sometime that spring, Edward joined the family. I suppose our parents hoped for another daughter, but I doubt if anyone was very disappointed. We were used to babies and life went on much the same with one more.

Crops were planted in great hopes of another good summer, and we tried not to see the remains of the burned barn. Our pa had stored some grain there and now we'd had to buy seed. We had lost some small haystacks next to the barn, too. As talk went on we realized that the fire had been quite a setback to the family economy. Little did we guess how much worse it would be. Late spring was as dry as it had been earlier.

Mother and we children planted the garden only to have the seeds blow away. Very little of anything came up. We stayed out of school to herd cattle so much that we finally gave up and dropped out for the summer. Most boys around were herding too, so we didn't get behind our class.

Even the Fourth of July wasn't as happy as it had been in years past. Almost everyone had a seven-shot shotgun in those days, and on July Fourth there was friendly competition to see who could get off his seven shots and wake the neighbors.

We were up early to hear the shooting. The silences in some directions reminded us that some of our friends had left the community. Pa had a contempt for those who gave up and left the homesteads. "No guts," he'd say. There was a joke that folks had to stay; they were too poor to leave. There may have been some truth to that.

Some crops came up in the spring only to shrivel and die in a hot, dry wind. Sometimes the wind would start with a rainy feel, and then turn dry and blow for days. This killed or severely retarded the young crops. Conditions such as this caused many homesteaders to leave the area.

Sometimes the neighbors were told and other times no one knew for days or weeks that a family or bachelor had deserted a claim. People usually took what they could haul in a wagon. Livestock may have been sold to pay bills, and machinery might have been mortgaged, so it was left for the bank or dealer. When a claim was left the neighbors grazed the land. Three or four men might get together and divide up things. It was agreed that this fellow take the shanty, "He has the biggest family."

Most shanties were ten- or twelve-feet square, so they made one more room. In many cases that doubled the size of a house. Small buildings were moved to become hog or hen houses. A soddy isn't movable, but windows and doors are. Anything usable was taken by someone. There were books, furniture, curtains or nothing left, depending on the kind of people and their circumstances at the time they left. Many also sold or gave away what they couldn't take or didn't want, unless they wanted to leave unnoticed.

Call it stealing if you like, but the homesteaders weren't well to do. Many had large families and the prairie didn't offer as good a living as many had been lead to hope for. The deserter had taken all he could and there was no use to let anything go to waste when others were in need. As soon as the bank or land agent learned that the claim was empty, he tried to get someone else on it to make it pay. So he liked to know before the neighbors stripped the premises. Not all who left the homesteads deserted in a run-away sense. Many bought the claim and then sold or leased it before going.

Let us not think badly of any of these people. Most of them really tried and few were failures for quitting the claim. Homesteading was the downfall of many, both economically and to their health.

The corn didn't sprout in 1911 and the small grains were killed by the hot winds. In early summer, the men were worried about hay. The stock were eating the grass as fast as it grew. What would be left to cut for hay? A farmer can sell or in some way cut down on the number of animals to be fed, but that does not help to build up a farm. If Pa let a team go he would be short of horse power.

If Pa sold cattle, he wouldn't have the replacement heifers to keep the herd growing. Thin poorly fed cows have weak calves and don't milk well. Besides, no one else had hay or feed, who would buy extra livestock? No crop meant no feed grain and no produce to sell or trade for the things we couldn't raise.

"You break up too much land, now you're short on pasture and hay," Mother said unhappily.

"Yah, yah," Pa barked. "Well, it won't always be so dry."

"That don't help now," grumbled our usually cheerful mother. "It'll be like in 1909 when you had to buy hay and we never had anything extra all winter."

That year, I recall was the time we had only one orange each for Christmas treats. Mother had made cookies before the hens had quit laying eggs. She hid those cookies so there would be something special for Christmas. How tired of bread and syrup sandwiches we would be next fall if we got no crop!

"Can we help?" I asked Christoff when we were alone.

"Can't make it rain," he said.

Pa came from town after chores and supper one evening and announced, "We'll have plenty of hay this winter, Mamas." I don't know how this pet name came about. Perhaps it is a distortion of some German word, but it was Pa's name for our mother and no one else called her "Mamas."

Mother was getting the little folks ready for bed. "What you mean?" she snapped. "With each day dryer than the last, and you say 'plenty of hay'?"

"We'll have hay," Pa repeated. "Know what some are doing? A bunch of guys are going up to North Dakota and cut hay. I'm going, too. The grass is high as your head there, right along the railroad. We'll just cut it and ship it home. The government will pay for part of the shipping. And they got a machine they call a baler. It makes a sort of ball of hay and ties it together. Men ride it and do the tying. Oh, everything will be fine, you'll see."

It was plain to see that Mother wasn't so sure. She had seen Pa's plans fall by the wayside before. "Can't make it worse," she muttered.

In a few days Pa left with mower and hay rake in the hay wagon, along with tools, grease and some spare parts. An extra team of horses trailed along tied to the rear of the hayrack. Mother packed a food box that looked like Pa wouldn't be near a kitchen for a month. And maybe he wouldn't.

The haying country was near Reeder, west of Hettinger, North Dakota, and about ninety miles from home.

Christoff and I were eleven and twelve that summer, and we and Mother were left with the responsibility of getting cattle to grass and water wherever we could find them, and of keeping up fence so the milk cows could be kept near home. We also had to see that water was pumped for hogs, other stock and house use. All feed, skim milk, and water for hogs was carried by bucket to the lot and dumped into a smelly, full-of-flies trough.

Sometimes we hitched old Fanny to the stoneboat and set pails of feed or milk on it to move across the yard. We rationed feed carefully and hogs were supposed to graze in their pasture. But when feed is scarce and grazing poor, livestock begin looking for a way out. We had pigs in the yard and in what was left of Mother's garden. I suppose Hilda and Louie had as much trouble with those hogs as Christoff and I did with the cattle.

Mother was a strong little woman, but she and we boys couldn't keep up fence or set posts in the hard-baked ground. We gave up and both herded cattle every day, bringing the whole herd so to have the milking herd home each evening. After a while Mother began to fear that the well would go dry, so we herded the stock to the Grand River each day and let them drink.

The best grazing land was along the river, but that was already taken, and some had crops on the lowlands. How we fought to keep stock out of the fields! Most of it was fenced, but that didn't always help. We had just one horse, old Fanny, between us, so one boy would ride and the other ran.

When Pa had asked us to manage things, he promised to try to get us a pony from up north. He had heard of herds of small horses up there. Louie especially asked for a spotted pony, but we older guys weren't particular about color. We had some doubt about getting anything to ride.

One hot day we herded all the way to the river only to find it gone completely dry. So we pumped stock water at home. A week or so later one of the neighbors stopped in to tell Mother that some men had dug a well and set up a pump in the river bed and we should water there if we wished. How relieved we were not to have to worry about using too much water from the home well.

We ate what we raised. We had eggs and milk and Mother's good bread that she baked two or three times a week in huge pans. Our mother cooked the old potatoes in the skins so we could use every bit. A few beans had come in the garden, watered by the house waste water. What a treat the fresh vegetables were! Boys get hungry for meat. If Pa were home he would kill a chicken. After talking about it for several days, Christoff and I told our mother that we wanted to butcher a chicken. With some difficulty we managed to kill two which Mother prepared for the table. I think we didn't enjoy the meal a great deal, but we knew we could get more meat if we had to.

With Pa gone so long, Mother baking often, and the weather turning chilly early as is often the case after a dry summer, we were running out of wood. We boys, or one of us and one of the smaller children, ranged out away from the farm picking up broken fence posts. Every scrap of lumber, corn cobs, and dry cow chips were on their way to the kitchen stove.

In October the hay was shipped to Lemmon and Pa was home. We still had much to do and we were out of school about half the time. We helped get a load of wood from along the river. And we helped fix up the fences so the stock would stay home.

Pa didn't want to feed hay any sooner than he had to, so we still herded cattle weekends and after school, and sometimes all day. One day we went with Pa to the Grand River and east where we dug our own coal. There is, or was, a layer of poor grade dusty lignite coal in the high bluff on the north side of the river. It was quite a chore to chip and pick-ax, then shovel on a wagon load of coal. But it was free for the digging and it was certainly better than no coal.

Pa had traded an older horse for a jack mule at the coal mines near Haynes. This was our promised "pony"! We couldn't hide our disappointment, but Jack was useful in one way. So many families had moved away that there weren't enough children to keep a school open. So our dads hauled all the desks and equipment to a deserted claim shanty on a bluff east of the Goedert place. This was about four miles from home and Hilda was too small to walk, so we drove the mule on the stoneboat to school.

There had been so many haying in North Dakota that the baling wasn't done on time, and the government removed the shipping rates before our pa could get finished and send the hay home. He had to hire baling and pay full freight costs. Pa made the fifteen mile trip to town almost every day. He had to have that hay home before the snow came or he still wouldn't have feed for the winter! Some hay was stored in the hay yard where stock could put their heads between poles and help themselves. Stacks appeared in the yard, and a few broken bales were tossed to hogs and chickens.

Sometimes Pa could haul two loads of hay in a day if he made the trip to town late the day before and stayed in overnight. These times we boys and Mother had to rise extra early to get chores done before school. Mother had been doing the harder milking cows, but we were old enough to be helping there; now one of us would sit down to the harder milkers. Some cows can almost milk themselves, while with others you have to fight for every drop. I expect we needed the cream badly to have kept milking some of those cows.

This seems the place to tell a little about the calves. A new calf would be left with his mother a few days. Then he was taken and put into a calf pen and taught to drink from a pail. We didn't have the nipple pails that many use now, so our calves were taught to drink with their heads down. This is not natural for a calf. Calves will suck on anything they can get into their mouths or it might be impossible to teach them. When a boy is tall enough, he climbs into the calf pen with part of a pail of warm milk (which will be cold shortly) and lets the calf get to sucking a couple of his fingers. Calves are born with teeth! Now gently ease the little guy's nose down into the milk in the pail. Of course he won't cooperate; he wants to reach up to suck.

The calf lets go the fingers and grabs your shirt tail. Boy straddles calf, offers fingers and tries again. Calf butts pail pinching fingers and boy considers fresh veal for supper. By now the milk is cold and you feed it to an older calf and get some fresh milk for the baby calf. Boy climbs into the pen, offers fingers, and backs calf into a corner to try easing calf's mouth into the pail.

If you're lucky and he's hungry, he'll drink a bit of milk around your sore fingers and begin to learn. If you aren't lucky or are a bit too light or short legged or the calf is extra ornery, he'll bolt out from under you, spilling you and the milk every which way. In a few weeks the baby graduated to hay, grain and skim milk. Big calves are as bad to feed because they are rough and greedy.

Mother got along well with cows and boys, and chores went best if she was there to cheer things along. Perhaps Pa was still hauling hay, or maybe he had gone for supplies, but one morning the wind came up and it began to snow hard while we were milking. When it was time to go to school our mother wouldn't let us go. "It is too far and if Pa don't get home, I have no help at all," she said. "Is bad enough I got to wonder if he's out in the storm without you all gone, too." We stayed home and played with the little folks and caught up on our rest and visited with Mother. Maybe she let us make fudge or popcorn later in the day. And we surely heard again the tale of the man in the snow bank.

Snow was still blowing around the buildings when it was time to do evening chores. Mother had decided not to look for Pa and that we must do the chores before dark. "There is a long rope in the cellar," Mother sent one of the small boys to get it. Chris and I got into our outdoor clothing.

Mother didn't ever own a pair of jeans, but in such weather, she would pull on a pair of Pa's overalls, stuffing her skirts down inside. Mother took the rope and tied it to the handle beside the door outside.

"Now we'll just follow it out and back." Mother put eight-year-old Hilda in charge of the house. "Hilda is boss; mind her. No one leaves the house, understand?" The little boys nodded.

Besides them, there was baby Eddy to look after. Mother took a last peek into the stove, then pails in hand, we stepped out into the swirling white. Snow stung our eyes and faces as we worked our way toward where the barn was supposed to be. We've missed it, I thought, we'll all be like the man in the snow.

"Hold tight and go slow," Mother yelled right beside me to make me hear. The dark form of the soddy barn loomed before us and we found the door and stumbled inside. Only Mother had sense enough to hold onto the rope. She carefully tied it to a post. Quickly as possible we did the work and stumbled out into the snow. What if the rope came untied from the house, I wondered. Soon we were safe at the door and gratefully flung ourselves inside.

Our clothing was stiff with the fine snow driven into the fabric and the milk was almost all blown from the pail full we had tried to bring in for drinking. "Mein Gott! What a night!" Mother looked around, "I think the wind be down later."

Mother was right. Morning was clear and very cold. Later that day, Pa got home and we all relaxed over a new Sears catalogue he had brought.

Catalogues played an interesting part in the lives of the settlers. It was our buyers' guide, price list, style book, department store, and finally it was carried to the outhouse for use there as toilet paper.

There was a time when almost anything could be ordered through the catalogues. Dried fruit in large wood boxes came at Christmas time, also candy, as well as shoes and clothing, sewing material, harness, tools, and furniture. Much of our clothing was ordered from the Sears catalogue.

Not this fall. Sears would be a wish book only. Or it would be a thankful book, depending on whether you were wishing for something or being thankful that you didn't need it. There just wasn't any extra cash.

As I said, it was a chilly fall. Mother cut down some old things of Pa's and Uncle Charlie's to make extra jeans and jackets for us boys who had to be outdoors so much. Such things often fit poorly, but we weren't concerned with that. We needed something warm.

When Mother cut out a garment she laid something that fit us over the new goods and cut around it giving a little extra for seams and to allow for our growth. Nothing was wasted; when a garment was outgrown, it was passed to the next smaller child. Worn out things were taken apart and made into quilt pieces or patches or cut down for a smaller child. Mother saved the buttons and sometimes the thread. The back of a worn out shirt became a diaper; a corner of a blanket went around the baby or into a new quilt. Cloth flour sacks became dish towels or diapers, or sewn together, made sheets. Anything beyond use was cut into strips and rolled into the rug rag ball. One day we would come home to find a new soft, hand braided rug beside our bed. What luxury to step out onto that rug in the morning!

"Yah," Pa said as Christmas neared, "it was a tough year, but we made it. We're all here and well and the homestead is ours."

-11-
HARD YEARS AHEAD

I hope my stories don't sound as though we worked and had trouble all the time. We had good times together around the community. Dances and parties were held in the homes during the less busy season and whole families went. Mothers took a cake or sandwiches to help with the lunch. Dancing, visiting, and games went on until dawn. Then those still up had breakfast and everyone went home, did chores and went to bed.

This was where we learned to dance. Dads taught the girls, and boys danced with mothers or sisters to get started. If we felt too young or uninterested, there were boys' games and girls' chattering groups to join. Some of the homes had pianos and someone who could play or chord along with the violins or guitars. Some of the fellows played harmonicas. I tried it myself when I was older but never got very good. We played mostly waltzes and such things as "Turkey in the Straw" and "Old Dan Tucker."

Old Dan Tucker was a fine old man,
He washed his feet in the frying pan,
Combed his hair with a wagon wheel,
And died of a tooth ache in his heel!
(Pum-pa-da-da-da! Clap-clap!)

Summer fun might be an evening ball game then an all-night dance, breakfast, chores and sleep most of Sunday. Having parties at home helped the mothers.

The problem of a tired and grouchy tot is solved by putting him to bed. I have seen six or so babes asleep on a bed together. In the next room several children would be sleeping on the floor only a few feet from the dancers and fiddlers.

Spring was hen setting time and extra work for Mother and Hilda. It also meant eggs and chickens for winter eating. The hens we kept were a meat type, larger and heavier than the nervous laying type. When a hen is ready to "set" and raise a family of chicks, she takes to a nest and ruffles her feathers and squawks rudely to anyone coming near. Setting hens have a mean way of pecking, even though they have no teeth!

The women chose a quiet, dark corner of a barn or granary, fixed a box or small barrel for each nest and set the hens. Each hen had her box and clutch of twelve or fourteen eggs. A light piece of board or screen covered the hen for a day or two. After that the hens kept to their nests except for the once a day when they were quietly fed and watered.

The hens warmed the eggs for the three weeks required for chicken eggs to hatch. As the time for the chicks to come neared, Mother or Hilda would look two or three times a day for new chicks.

The tiny fluffy babies were taken to the house and put in a box near the stove. They must have an old towel or something to crawl under. It is necessary to take the first chicks because as soon as they can get around, the hen will leave the nest and let the rest of her eggs cool, killing the unhatched chicks. After all the eggs had hatched, the hen and her brood were moved into a little coop or hutch made of scrap wood or a large barrel. This was done to keep them out of the rain and a little safe from skunks, cats, and badgers.

Slats were put across the front of the coop for a couple days and the chicks, tiny balls of yellow or brown fluff, ran in and out to please themselves. One warm sunny day, Mother would open the door and let the hen out. How proudly she would strut about showing off her family! We shooed the hens in each night and closed the coops until the dew was dry next morning. Hens and chicks lived in the little coops until the chicks were big enough to take care of themselves.

Then the hen would go back to the laying coop of her own accord and the chicks would gather around the little house and chirp in a lonesome way for a few nights. I have seen a sympathetic old rooster move in with chicks at this time. Maybe he only came for the extra feed. Tom cats can be death on young chicks, but I recall a large orange one staying with well grown chicks after their mother left them. They only shared the warmth of each other's bodies a short while, but I'm sure the cat didn't harm those big chicks. The young chickens soon found the hen house and thereafter lived with the rest of the flock.

From ten to fifty broods of chicks were raised in this way each summer. We got goose eggs and turkey eggs from various sources and the hens incubated them and raised the young. A chicken hen is a better mother than a turkey and she never knows the difference until the young are old enough to get along without her. A hen mothering ducks or geese when they start swimming is a sight indeed!

Chickens will forecast the weather. On a rainy day the hens will stay out pecking around if it will be an all-day thing. But if it's just a shower you will see the hens run for shelter.

Young roosters learning to crow is one of the funnier memories for any farm youth. If you haven't heard this, I'm afraid you won't appreciate why I think it's worth mentioning. The young fellows try to mimic the old red rooster when he gives his morning call from a post or other high spot.

The leggy half-grown roosters do a lot of wing flapping and strutting and often throw themselves off balance before they even get around to try crowing. Then with much neck stretching and eye rolling, they come out with a strange series of squawks and chuckles, a far cry from the loud and proud "cock-a-doodle-do" they are trying for. After this the young bird will often attack another as though it were his fault.

This summer when Chris was thirteen and I was near twelve, Uncle Charlie told us that he was planning to return to Minnesota. "To work?" we asked.

"I'm selling and going to move. This country is too much for me," he said.

"Why? Are we all going? Are Ma and Pa going?"

"Now don't worry about it," our uncle tried to soften the news. "You are big boys and one day you will each have a farm like your pa wants. You took care of things last summer without us. Why, you're men already!" He went hurriedly about some work.

Somehow Uncle Charlie doesn't fit into that summer. He probably was in Minnesota then.

As we talked about this turn of events, we each tried to make the other guy feel better. But the fun was gone out of the summer. One day we heard Uncle Charlie say he would stay to see his niece.

We suspected that there would be a baby at our home. Parents and children didn't talk about such things, so we pretended we didn't know and our parents pretended we hadn't guessed.

Before much longer we learned that our parents had bought Uncle Charlie's claim. They bought everything except personal items. The twelve-by-twelve foot shanty would become a bunk house for us boys.

This was moved and our uncle stayed with us while he finished his business. We boys had had a summer bedroom on the screened east porch the past summer, but this was a greater treat. Even the fact that we would have to build a fire morning and evening didn't dim our pleasure. It might have when winter came! We slept in the house the next winter when it was very cold. After that the bunk house served boys and hired men.

This fall there was school at the soddy again and a couple of fathers took wagons and hauled desks and other things back from the shanty on the bluff. Mr. Keller was probably our teacher.

Louie began school in 1912 and Mother had a new problem at home. It seems that little Billy would be so busy in his play that he wouldn't bother to answer Mother when she called to see what he was doing and if he was safe. Mother would call, "Billy! Billy, where are?" and get no reply, though he might be just around the corner. Mother was so afraid that he might come upon a rattlesnake in his play. "Here we have the bad snakes and a no-good dog," she grumbled, remembering her pet, Jack. Well she might worry; there were a lot of rattlesnakes in the area.

One day both our parents scolded Billy. "When Mamas calls you, you say 'What?' so she knows you didn't fall in the tank and drown!" Pa ordered the little guy. After that when Mother told something he had said or done, three-year-old Billy stood by asking, "What, Mama, what?" That went on only for a short while, but it is something I remember about Bill when he was small.

We came from school one day to find Mrs. Hoefling or another helpful neighbor there and we knew that baby Lester had come. Mother had her hands full. Billy was three, Eddy a year-and-a-half old, and now a new baby. Pa wasn't much help with an infant. Once in a while, if someone would put the baby on a pillow, Pa would hold the pillow for a few minutes. But if the baby cried or fussed, he would say, "Here, Mamas, take your baby."

Uncle Charlie left before Christmas, promising to write to us and come to visit. We who didn't get back to Minnesota, never saw him again.

Quite naturally the Millers had the New Year's dance. How could Mother take her brood anywhere in winter? Besides the three little boys, Louie must have been seven; Hilda, nine; I, twelve and Christoff would have been thirteen.

-12-
GOODBYE, CHRISTOFF, 1913

The only thing that stands out in my mind from the year 1913 is losing my brother. That was late in the year, so first I would like to tell about our stoves and the cream separator.

Kitchen stoves, or ranges came in styles and sizes from the small one with four lids on top and no warming oven or reservoir to the six- or eight-lidded size with huge water reservoir and large overhead warming ovens. All had ovens next to the ash pan, stove pipes running up the back, and sturdy legs about fourteen inches long. Most stoves had a reservoir, a square water container that hung on the end opposite the fire box.

A few had them at the hot end with the fire box in the middle and the oven at the other side. The reservoir had a lid that we opened to pour in the two to six pails of water needed to fill it. This was our hot water heater and we used a dipper to take out the water as needed. The reservoir also served as a humidifier, something we didn't know we needed. The tea kettle stood on the back of the stove and its singing was a cheerful sound.

Another type of stove was called a monkey stove. This was low and flat and had no oven, only a cook top. Uncle Charlie had one something like that in the bunk house. They were used in some schools and temporary homes.

There was a round potbellied heater that burned large chunks of wood or coal. We had one in the frame house and at school.

In the two-room soddy, the kitchen range heated the entire house. We gathered around to dress in its warm glow in the early morning, and after supper we sat as near as was comfortable as we did our lessons. Pa sat with his feet on the open oven door warming himself after a day out in the weather. The opened door made a warm spot to take a quick bath or to dry mittens.

The range heated water for laundry, canning and the scalding of hogs at butchering time. All this took a lot of fuel and kept the house hot and steamy. In the 1920s and 1930s, Mother would have a two burner kerosene stove for meal-time cooking in the summer. But it was still the wood range for heating large amounts of water or doing the baking.

The stoves sat out from the walls, and behind was piled wood sawed the proper length to fit the fire box and then split lengthwise with an ax. A box of chips, scraps from the chopping and corn cobs if we had them, sat nearby or under the reservoir.

This was also the wastebasket as all trash was used for fire starting. The ash pan slid into a door below the fire and the ashes fell through a grate into the pan. When an ash pan is less than full is the best time to empty it. That would be twice a day in cold weather. Each spring Mother would get Pa or a couple of boys to help and down came the stove pipes for their annual cleaning. The pipes were carefully carried outside where the accumulation of soot was pounded from them. We usually ran a pipe right up to the chimney, but in the old days folks often put the stove across the room from the chimney and ran pipes along under the ceiling. The pipe was held by wires fastened to staples in the ceiling.

It was thought that less heat escaped. Since heat rises, it was wasted anyway unless someone slept in the attic. A hot pipe near the ceiling may well have caused a fire for someone. And think of the poor women who had all this dusty apparatus to clean!

Fairly early in the history of the farm, our pa got a cream separator. This machine saved Mother the time consuming chore of cooling and skimming milk. "How does it work?" we wanted to know as the heavy thing was carried down into the storm cellar.

Pa had read about separators in a farm magazine before he invested in one. "You know how the cream rises to the top in the crocks because it is lighter than the milk? Well, it rises in the separator for the same reason. It floats. Only now it will take a few minutes and not all day and night," he explained.

The works of a separator consist of a bowl, which contains a number of light metal disks. There is a heavy iron cover over this pyramid shaped part, and a nut at the top to hold it all together. This is taken apart and washed every day or so. Our pa impressed us with the importance of getting the bowl together correctly and of having the nut tight, lest it come apart and fling steel disks every which way. There are two spouts, one to carry cream to its container, and the other to run skimmed milk into a bucket. The supply tank holding three to eight gallons of milk sits way up on top.

A cloth strainer was fastened with clothes pins to the rim of the tank. There is always some straw, hair, and dust clinging to a cow, any of which will fall into the milk pail. (Maybe more often when kids milk.) So it was important to strain the milk well. The cloth was washed twice a day.

Then come the milkers with pails of fresh milk. One of the bigger lads takes the crank and begins winding up the machine. This is quite hard work depending on the size of the machine and the size of the boy.

Others pour milk through the strainer into the tank, being sure first that the faucet is closed. It is a mess if the milk comes into the machinery too soon and runs out all over. If the crank is turned too fast, the cream will be very thick and there won't be much. The idea is to turn fast enough to get the cream, but not to get it too thin. When the separating was finished, a gallon or more of water was run through the machinery to rinse it as the whirling parts slowed to a stop. In hot weather Mother washed the separator every day, but in cold weather it could be let go several days.

With a bigger farm, our pa could justify more machinery and this spring he bought a lister, a combined corn planter-plow drawn by a team of horses. Until now we had planted corn by hand. We didn't plant a lot of corn since the short season varieties hadn't come along. Our dad had farmed Iowa and raising corn in Dakota was just his kind of challenge.

We got a one-row cultivator, too. This worked like the walking plow with the farmer driving the team and machine as he walked behind. Before many days, eight-year-old Louie found his place riding the cultivator tongue and driving the horses so Pa could give his full attention to guiding the cultivator. We enjoyed not having to hoe corn and potatoes anymore.

One summer Pa got a washing machine for Mother. There was a round wooden tub with a hand-turned wringer held by brackets to the side. There was a dasher of wood in the center of the tub. A boy was required to push and pull a handle that made the blade push the load of laundry back and forth and hopefully clean it. How tiresome that was! I expect that wasn't as hard for us as rubbing clothing on a washboard had been for our mother, but we'd have rather done almost any outdoor work. Soon Mother was using her rub-board in the tub and using the wringer while it lasted.

Christoff began having trouble when he was walking behind a drag in the springtime. As summer wore on, he spent more and more time in pain. We weren't encouraged to dwell on problems, so he probably worked along and tried to be cheerful when he didn't feel well at all. Late in the summer, Christoff had a really bad spell. After a couple days of home treatment, our pa rode into Lemmon and brought out young Dr. Totten who had come to Perkins County in about 1910.

Dr. Totten said the boy must be taken to Mobridge immediately. There was more or less of a hospital in Lemmon, but the doctor was alone. Operating by himself, the good man had lost a Hoefling child that spring. So Pa, the doctor, and Christoff hastily left in the buggy. I remember Mother crying and saying, "I'm afraid you won't be back, son."

"Now, Ma, I'll be back good as new," Chris had assured her. Mother was right. Dr. Totten went along on the train to Mobridge, but Christoff died of a ruptured appendix shortly before or soon after arriving at the hospital there.

A broken-hearted Pa came home to tell us the sad story. The German Lutheran pastor refused to hold services because we hadn't been to church regularly. Pa had gone to a Presbyterian minister and found help and sympathy. Christoff was laid away in the Lemmon cemetery, and my childhood ended.

The greatest blow to my youth, perhaps to my entire lifetime, was my brother's death. We were pals, sharing work and fun. I could hardly face life without him. I had always thought that I worked the same as Christoff did, but when I was called upon to fill his shoes, how hard it was! Louie, five years younger than I, had the same trouble trying to fill my former station in the family work force. How lazy and helpless he seemed to me.

I was too young and unhappy to see that he no doubt was doing all a boy his age could do. If our parents noticed that we were having trouble, they said or did nothing to help. They had their own work, worry and grief to contend with. People just weren't aware of children's feelings then.

Christmas of 1913 was the saddest of my life. My brother was gone, Uncle Charlie had left, the ponds and creeks were dry so there was no trapping.

The buffalo bones had been picked, so we had no means of making even a small amount of change. The crop hadn't been poor, but there were expenses from Chris's illness and death, and all that machinery to pay for.

No one was in any mood for Christmas, but what was worst to me was when Louie and I tried to help Pa bring in a cow soon to calve. The stubborn animal ran past the barn door several times. "Get a stick!" Pa yelled. So I found sticks for both us boys. Louie wouldn't take his. The poor boy stood shivering with his hands in his pockets and tears running down his face. Finally the fool cow was in the barn, then our Pa came out with a terrible oath and said no man should have to get so mad on Christmas Day. If I ever had such a Christmas since then, I was older and better able to handle it, so it didn't seem as bad as that one.

Probably because of the pastor's attitude, Hilda and I were enrolled in confirmation class. We drove into town every week for instruction in the German Lutheran faith. Mother was disappointed in the narrow-minded views of this particular pastor and would have had us go to the Presbyterian Church.

This would be more like her family's United Brethren upbringing. "The poor man is crazy," Mother once said when we repeated his remarks concerning other churches. But I guess he was only doing his job as he saw it.

Hilda and I were confirmed in a class of three. Hilda had a new white dress and all the trimmings and I had a new suit and shoes. This was my first long pants dress up suit. We wore long pants for school and work, but dress up trousers were the baggy knee type worn with long dark socks. Since that day, both Hilda and I have left the Lutheran church, she to the Catholic and I to the Methodist.

Both of our parents were buried by the Lutheran Church, the easier to live with church of today.

This seems a good place to tell about the care of the ill in the early days. One home remedy that I recall for colds was a chest plaster made of sulfur and lard or goose fat. Some even used skunk fat! Folks thought the more disagreeable the remedy, the more good it did. That did discourage one from thinking he was ill if he wasn't! Sulfur came in a yellow powder and was mixed with warm fat and rubbed onto the chest. A cloth was heated on the stove pipe and laid over the poultice under the pajama or shirt.

When we had stomach flu, Mother boiled milk and cooled it for us to drink. We were encouraged to eat and keep up our strength. "You got to eat," Pa would say. But meat and potatoes don't taste good then, and we didn't have the Jello and sauce like now. We didn't have the fresh fruits and vegetables, yet we ate quite well even in bad years.

There were no window screens and no way to keep flies out of the house and away from food and dishes. Barns and outhouses were often near the house. There were no refrigerators, only the storm cellar and cans of cool or cold water in which to store and chill foods. It is a wonder that we weren't ill more often.

Castor oil was a much used and over-used remedy in many homes. It was thought that laxative would remove poisons from the system. It surely caused some dehydration, much grief, and perhaps even ruptured appendixes. It could take one's mind off whatever else ailed him!

Sore or stiff muscles were rubbed with strong smelling, oily liniment. Cuts were treated with iodine which burned like everything, or they were ignored. Many folks dipped a cloth in vinegar, squeezed it out and laid it across the forehead of those with a headache. One Russian lady sliced potatoes and laid the slices on the sick person's forehead. She tied a cloth around the head to keep the potato slices in place. Some agreed that it was a good remedy, that it "drew out" the pain. I don't believe we ever tried that at home.

Butter was put on burns and many believed you should hold a burn over heat "to take out the soreness." How that hurt! Cough syrup was made from onions and honey. A slice of onion laid under the pillow was supposed to relieve a stuffed nose as the cold sufferer slept. At times it did, or seemed to. We were given a quarter teaspoon of kerosene along with three times as much sugar to stop a coughing fit. The Russian neighbor once said that her kids were raised "on the kerosene bucket."

If someone fell and bruised himself, we ran to get a silver dollar or a table knife and held the metal against the bump. Some thought that silver had a healing power, but it was the coolness and the pressure that helped keep the bump down.

Once Pa mashed a thumb in some machinery. He made a "finger stall" of some stiff paper or light cardboard, filled it with axle grease, and pushed the thumb in. Mother wrapped the case with cloth and tied it up to Pa's hand to keep it on. The thumb healed.

There was a hospital open in Lemmon off and on after 1910, but long after that women continued to have babies at home. A neighbor woman came in to help the mother after the babe was born, and she might come the next day to help out if there wasn't a girl there big enough to do dishes and such. The good ladies had their own homes and families to care for. Some of these were Mrs. Hoefling and Mrs. Wheaton. In the 'teens, a family of Frerkings moved in west of us. This woman was a helpful neighbor and near enough to come in a few minutes.

Burns and broken bones posed some of the most serious problems to the homesteaders. There is a sad story about a little boy who had been badly burned by hot water or maybe by grease. He was ill for a long time, but finally his parents began to think he was getting better. One night as the little lad was being readied for bed, he said, "I think I'm going to die tonight." The parents tried to tell him that he was getting better, but he did sleep away that night. This was told to us to help us understand how important it was to be careful not to get burned.

We must have been very well trained and cautious concerning the snakes. None of the family had any bad experience, or at least none was bitten by a rattlesnake.

We did hear of a man who died of a snake bite, and sometime later the wife remarried. The new husband took and wore the first man's boots. Before long he developed a sore on his heel. This man fell ill and died. A son grew up to the boots and took them to wear. He noticed a pricking at the heel. A close look revealed part of a rattlesnake fang imbedded in the leather. It was supposed that the fang held some dry venom, and when it had worked a sore, the moisture of the foot has carried the poison into the blood stream. The son? I hope he burned the boots.

-13-
CHANGES, 1914

When spring came in 1914 we were forced to gather our wits and go about the business of spring work. Pa found a man to help with the plowing and planting. We did quite a lot of fencing, but there would be herding to do for years yet. The farm was growing, both in crop land and in several quarters leased or rented as pasture and hay land.

The hired man shared the bunk house with me or with Louie and me. It was one of these fellows who taught us a stunt that I have enjoyed with my grandsons: Get the fellows to stand in a circle, one ahead of the next. Then everybody sits down on the next guy's inside knee. Several boys, or in this day, girls, too, can sit quite comfortably for a minute or until someone gets funny and spills everybody.

One hired man was quite a disappointment to me. I don't recall that we didn't get along, but once he made me feel awfully bad. When Mother served cake, we children liked to slice ours crosswise and save the top with its fudge frosting for last.

I had done this and set the special treat at the side of my plate. Before I was finished with the first part the man reached over and took my cake. He ate it up without a word!

I was cleaning the milking barn one day that spring or summer when a car came chugging down the road and turned in at our gate. Cars were a rare sight, especially in the country in 1914. Seeing me standing in the door with wide eyes, - and mouth, no doubt - the man drove directly to the barn. He asked where to find my pa. I began to explain what field and how to get there. "Why don't you just hop in and show me?" our caller invited. "That's easier."

I hesitated, wondering if I shouldn't let Mother know I had gone. A glance toward the house told me she would be hearing very soon from the staring children gathered at the door. The man smiled and opened the door and I got in. As we rode to the field he talked to me in a friendly man-to-man way about the family and the farm. Perhaps he knew and perhaps he didn't, but he was giving me one of the greatest thrills of my young life. Ten years later I went up in a small plane at a fair, but it wasn't as exciting to me as that first car ride.

This might be a good place to mention foods. Our summer diet included lots of eggs and if we had it, salt meat, old potatoes, and whatever vegetable there was. When the corn was ready we ate roasting ears every day. Now with a home freezer you can have fresh vegetables any time. Not so then. Roasting ears were really a treat! All our vegetables were home grown in those years. We raised the usual beans and peas in good years. If we could afford seed, some radishes and lettuce was planted. You can save these seeds if you want to bother. Mother probably did.

Carrots and turnips were stored in dry sand in pails in the storm cellar or in the small one under the house. Potatoes were hand dug or plowed out and picked up to be piled in the yard to dry. Then they were bagged or poured loose into a bin in the cellar.

Ripe beans, peas and corn can be shelled, dried in a cloth bag on the clothes line, and stored indoors all winter. These hard vegetables must be soaked overnight before cooking.

Pumpkins and squash will keep well stored in oats or straw, and they are not taking up needed storage space in the house or cellar. We probably used them up by Christmas. Mother saved seed from these as well as melon and cucumber seeds if we were lucky enough to raise some. Cucumbers were made into pickles and kept in a brine barrel. When we wanted some pickles, someone would go down and rinse off a few. By late winter that brine was getting thick and rank smelling.

We often stored eggs in a pail of oats for a few months. Hens didn't lay in the winter, and by greasing the eggs and storing them there would be a few for Christmas baking and perhaps for some cookies and cakes during the winter.

We always had homemade bread, cornbread, pancakes, and plenty of milk. We ate clabber - cold clabbered milk. This is raw milk gone past the sour stage. Pasteurized milk will not clabber, but raw milk will become thick, almost like cheese, and it takes on a sweet-sour flavor. We sprinkled sugar over chunks of clabber and ate it cold from the cellar with a spoon. (It was a lot like yogurt.)

The women made cottage cheese from the skimmed milk. This was done by heating the sour milk slowly to a certain temperature. The milk solids rose to the top leaving the yellowish liquid called whey. A pan of milk might stand on the cooler end of the range all day before reaching the proper consistency.

Mother then strained or dipped off the cheese with her cream skimmer, the nearly flat spoon-shaped tool used for skimming cream from the cooled milk before we got the cream separator. The skimmer had many holes punched in it to let the milk or whey drain back. Homemade cottage cheese is dryer than what you buy.

We mixed a little milk or cream into the cheese and poured a bit of corn syrup on before eating it. Some like it with salt and pepper. We used a lot of cane or corn syrup. It may have been cheaper than sugar; it could be closed against such pests as ants and mice more easily, and syrup isn't affected by dampness as sugar is. Syrup came in a gallon pail with a tight lid and a wire handle.

The syrup pails were handy for lots of things like school lunches, taking water to men in fields, carrying eggs, and storing lard or cream. The syrup pitcher was always on the table. We used syrup on bread as well as on pancakes and cornbread. I like what we called "bachelor pie." Take a slice of bread, homemade is best, on the plate, pour a bit of milk or cream along the crusts, and top it with plenty of syrup. Instant dessert!

Before refrigeration, the keeping of meat was a problem. We ate an occasional chicken during the summer, but as soon as it was cool in the fall a hog was butchered. How good it was to growing boys to have meat to eat!

Mother made use of almost every scrap. All the fat was carefully rendered for lard. Fat is slowly cooked in the oven or on top of the stove until the melted lard leaves the meat scraps. Great care must be taken not to allow the lard to get too hot or to spatter on the stove and burst into flame. Many people have been burned by grease. Rendering lard was a tiresome and hazardous chore especially with small children in the house. The lard was stored in the pails, large jars, and crocks.

Tiny bits of meat left from the rendering of lard were called "cracklings" and they made a welcome variety in the flavor of pancakes, cornbread, and muffins. No, they aren't greasy, more like bits of well cooked bacon.

The smaller cuts of meat like chops were fried or roasted and then covered with lard and stored in a stone crock in the cellar. Most everyone had a small smoke house where meat was hung and a slow smoky fire kept going for days. We had ham, bacon, sausage and sometimes other cuts smoked.

Mrs. Wagner was good with meats and she often came and helped our mother make head cheese and sausage.

Before Christmas or soon after, when we could spare an animal, a beef was butchered. We chose a spot where the snow was clean and dragged the meat on the snow as we worked. We kept moving into a clean area. This would be just too much for the health inspectors today! We were careful and the meat was well cooked. Much field dressed game is not as well cared for as that meat. This could be cut and stored in a barrel until we used up the hard frozen meat.

If it didn't get warm too early in the years when we were many mouths to feed, we had another hog to eat in the spring. Gradually Mother got more canning jars and some meat could be canned for summer use.

Canning of the vegetables was done on the cook stove each summer in the late 1920s and 1930s. Old-fashioned canning meant three hours of in a boiling water bath for safety. Mother probably canned fifteen or eighteen jars at once in a wash boiler. This meant lots of wood burning in the range and a hot and steamy kitchen. Later, women got large round canning kettles, and still later, pressure cookers that cut boiling time. The women canned vegetables, fruit, meat, jelly, and even milk by these methods, burning wood, cobs or cow chips in the range.

One fall job we boys liked was herding cattle. Sometimes we had the whole herd and sometimes just the stock cattle while the milk cows were in the fenced pasture. Harvested fields and creek beds offered good grazing for a month or so before snow fell. In the spring we might herd to save the pasture for summer. Herding meant a day off from school so we would take along a book which we were expected to use. More fun was practicing up on our riding skills.

We all tried anything we heard of and there was keen competition among the neighbor boys. This gave us a chance to get a day ahead of the other guys. We learned to run beside our loping pony and jump on, sit astride a moment, climb or hop off the other side, bounce high, remount, all at a gallop. Some of the fellows clambered under the horses' necks or bellies at a canter. We must have gotten scratched and stepped on, but we continued the games for years. I did let a horse fall with me once and broke my collar bone in the spill. That was later, after I was old enough to know better than to let a horse run downhill after dark.

We practiced until we could stand up on the saddle at a lope. We would then turn around to face the horse's tail. Some of us could stand on our heads in the saddle. We started at a walk and worked up to a trot and into a lope. It helps if you have a calm horse with a good gait. You have to earn his trust.

We trained our horses to stand and we ran up behind them, put our hands on their hips, and leaped into the saddle. If the horse doesn't trust you, you can get into real trouble doing that!

Once we were herding near the Hoefling farm about six miles north and west of the homestead. We saw Mr. Hoefling in the field and he told us to go to his place to water stock if we got near there. We moved the herd into his yard and found the stock water tank level full. It wasn't long until the four girls came out and informed us that they had just pumped that water and invited us to take ourselves and our cattle elsewhere. They were some pretty angry girls that day! We teased and kidded them awhile and then refilled the tank. They had no way of knowing their dad had invited us to water there.

This may be a good place to tell of the spelling bees held in the late fall and winter. The get-togethers were at the school and organized by the teacher. This was a change from dances and card parties. Sometimes a neighboring school came and the groups of students competed, or local students spelled against older brothers and sisters or parents.

Often everybody who wanted to compete against everyone else who wanted to spell joined in. The spellers would line up across the room and the teacher would begin with a long or tricky word. If the first speller missed the word he sat down and the next in line or the other team as the case may be, got to try it. If the word was spelled correctly there was a new word for the next speller and the first contestant stayed for the next round. Some of us sat down soon and others stayed a long time. The audience was quiet, listening for mistakes. Help was forbidden, but clapping and cheering were the order of the day. The bee might go on for an hour if there were several good spellers in the crowd. Other times a good speller or team was declared the champion and had everyone else "spelled down" quite soon. Tension ran high when it came to a contest between two very good spellers as one after the other they spelled long and tricky words.

After this entertainment the mothers unpacked coffee and cake. People talked and laughed, enjoying a chance to visit with the neighbors until late.

Our little sister, Ella, was born in 1914. With four brothers, this must have been a thrill to Hilda. I guess our mother might have given up hope of getting another daughter. Baby Ella did much to add to our Christmas spirit that winter. Whatever else, it was better than the past Christmas.

-14-
COMPANY, 1915

We were at supper after chores one evening in late spring when the dog barked. "Pa's coming," several voices said. We left our plates of clabber milk and bread to help with unloading the wagon.

When the team had been watered and put to pasture and groceries and supplies stored, Pa patted his shirt pocket. "I got something for you, Mamas," he teased before he handed her a letter.

Mother was nursing the baby. "You read for us," she said to Hilda. So the rest of us sat quietly while Hilda read the letter aloud.

Before Hilda got far into the letter, Mother repeated, "Oh, your cousin, Marie, and her new husband are coming to see us! And her folks, my sister, Anna, and Uncle Charles Graphenteen. You remember them? Henry? Hilda?" We nodded. Marie and Rose had come to our home to help Mother when we were little. "What else does it say?" Mother prodded.

"We are trying to talk Grandma and Grandpa Lang into coming along," Hilda read from the letter.

"Ach! Oh my! Then you got to practice the German so you can talk to them. What will they think? We got a bunch here can't talk "the German!" Mother fussed.

"Read that part again. Does it say we should let them know if it's handy for us?" Pa asked. Hilda and I bent over the letter and established that the relatives in Pipestone expected an answer. "Better now than in harvest," Pa said.

"The weather's still cool and the garden is good. We might have new vegetables," Mother put in. "Can you write yet tonight for me, Hilda?" She turned to Pa, "Maybe Henry could ride in to town with a letter?" Pa sucked at his pipe and nodded. Mother rose to put the sleeping baby to bed. Hilda looked around for a paper and pencil left from the school term just ended.

"To bed, you guys," Pa ordered the boys. He turned to me, "You go right after you bring up the cows in the morning. There's enough to help Mamas milk. Don't dawdle around, we still work here, you know." I nodded.

Next morning, it was my privilege to be riding across the grassy prairie toward Lemmon. I had gotten up with the early sun, saddled a horse, and looked up the milking herd. I found the cows lying along the creek and hustled them up and headed for home. Often it is a pleasure to let cows amble along, but this morning I pushed them as much as I dared. Our Pa didn't like us to hurry the cows it made them nervous and they couldn't "let down the milk."

Mother was standing at the door when I rode up to the house. "I laid out some clean clothes for you," she said. "Have something to eat now; want some eggs?" Just coffee and bread was fine, I told her.

I knew she'd have to make pancakes for the family after chores. I changed clothes and washed up a bit while the coffee cooled. From the bunk house I could see Pa getting ready to cultivate corn. Shortly before now we had gotten a new riding-type corn cultivator, and he was very proud of the machine.

Soon I was on my way to town and could enjoy the beautiful morning and the sturdy little horse who seemed to look forward to the trip as much as I did.

Gophers scampered along the trail, and meadowlarks called cheerfully from tall bunches of grass. I grinned as I thought of the two men named Pike and Litcherman. Mother had said that the meadowlarks' call said, "Here live Pike and Litcherman."

I was amused by the silly carrying on of the prairie dogs. A prairie dog is a lot like a gopher or a chipmunk; he's a relative of the squirrels.

Prairie dogs live in holes in the ground. The little creatures build up a ring of hard-picked earth around their underground homes. A prairie dog "town" may cover several acres and hold seventy or more dens. The little brownish-grey animals stand tall on the mound of earth outside the dens and yap like tiny dogs. As you come closer the little rodents dive into their holes. Then if you are quiet, you might see them come peeping out.

Once past the holes made by the prairie dogs, we could hurry more. We topped a little rise, and I could see the tall plume of smoke that indicated a train was in town. Lemmon seemed a quiet place on a weekday morning. I was used to seeing the Saturday shoppers if I got to town at all. There were only a couple of teams and buggies in sight. Dr. Totten's automobile stood in front of his office. I could see the drays, heavy freight wagons that hauled supplies and food stuffs from the train to the stores.

Under one of the drays lay a huge bulldog. I had seen him many times. Our pa had told us how on at least one occasion another dog had come too close to the wagon and the bulldog had attacked. The drayman climbed down and stuck a stick through his dog's collar and twisted it until the dog had to open his jaws and let the other go. He said that was the only way he could keep his dog from choking the other. Everyone gave that fellow plenty of room, and you may be sure nothing was ever taken from that wagon!

There was pounding at the blacksmith shop where some folks had their horses shod. Well, I better not even stop this morning or I would be late getting home. I rode to the post office. I had kept a hand near my pocket all the way to make sure I didn't lose Mother's letter.

I paid for the two-cent stamp, licked it, and pounded it tight. The postmaster smiled as he took the letter. "That will go east tonight," he said. "No mail, your pa got it yesterday," he added. I nodded and went out into the bright sunshine. I wondered if Mr. Miller, who was no relation, knew all the boys as he seemed to know me. I crossed to the grocery and bought a few cents' worth of lemon drops. I ate a couple while I watered my horse at the wooden trough in the middle of the street. Then I mounted and turned south.

It may or may not have been on this trip that I saw antelope, but the story would not be complete without something about the beautiful and bothersome western antelope. Anyone who hasn't seen them in action has missed a sight. The goat-like animals are brown or buff in color with white marking on the face, neck, underside, rump and legs. Antelope run in herds of five to twenty animals. Far away on a hill, you might catch sight of several playing and skipping around. You may be sure that they have long since decided how far away you are, how fast, and in what direction you are traveling, and probably whether or not you carry a gun.

Antelope are bothersome. They do great damage to haystacks, grain shocks, and corn fields if they are running the range in large numbers, or especially if there is ice or snow and they cannot get at their natural food supply. Antelope are good eating and their speed and agility make them a challenge to even the modern hunter.

Horses always travel faster on the way home, so we got there in time for the noon meal and the afternoon's work. The children were happy for the treat of a few pieces of hard candy.

Ten days or two weeks later Pa brought a letter saying when our company would come. Mother began planning for sleeping space for four or six extra people. It seems that our grandparents hadn't yet decided to come, but we had been practicing our German for them.

Mother cleaned and baked along with fixing beds in the bunk house, both bedroom and living room in the house, and the east porch outdoor bedroom. We boys and Pa would take straw ticks to the barn. Ticks were the cloth cases often stuffed with hair, feathers, or straw, and used for mattresses.

Talk was renewed about the Lang family and Mother tried to refresh our memories concerning the people we might have forgotten since we had left Minnesota in 1907. Mother told us in German how her father had insisted that the family walk the mile to church so the horses could rest on Sunday. We were to figure out the story and translate it to her. "They work all week," our grandpa said. But when he moved to town in later years, he put a tight rein on his horses and forced them into a brisk trot with heads held high. People called him "the doctor" for that.

Grandpa Lang is said to have stowed away aboard ship to get to America. It was many years before he learned that one of his brothers had also come to this country. The immigration rules must not have been as strict as later when my father came. We who could remember our cousins, Marie and Rose, and Aunt Anna looked forward to seeing them again. If only Grandpa and Grandma would come, we said to each other. And we kept practicing "the German."

I came from the field after raking hay all day. Mother and perhaps Louie had met the train to bring our company to the farm. The evening milking was being done with Mother, Louie and Hilda at the job.

I was mildly embarrassed that Mother would be milking when we had company, weren't there enough boys in the family? I unhitched my machine, unharnessed the horses, and turned them to pasture for the night. I paused only a moment to watch the animals roll in the dust and shake themselves before I stepped into the shady, darkish lean of the barn. "I'll help here, Ma you go up to the house. You got company," I suggested.

"You go say 'hello' first," she said. "I'm just going to finish this one. Pa just came from the mowing. Go now!" Mother insisted. "They'll think you don't know how to act."

We didn't argue with Mother, so I walked south past the house to join Pa and the company where the men were leaning on the fence and admiring the young pigs. I was proud to have someone see our farming operation. We had had good rains and the crops looked promising. "Knee high by the Fourth of July" was the old rule for judging corn. Barring hot dry winds or hail, ours would make it. The buffalo grass doesn't stay green like the Minnesota grasses, but it is nourishing, and our cows and calves were in good condition. Yes, they would be favorably impressed.

"Well, Henry!" exclaimed my cousin Marie, "You've grown up." I grinned bashfully, wishing I'd swung by the water tank and cleaned up a bit. Marie came and took my hand. I used to think she was a big girl, but now that we were both grown, she was a shorty.

"Otto, come and meet Henry," she called. Her husband, Otto Schuldt, came smiling and shook my hand. A man not afraid of dirt, I thought, liking him right away.

"I like your team," he said. "They work good together, don't they? Still look good after a day's work, too," he observed. I like horses, so a man who notices them has already scored with me. I was pleased that Mr. Schuldt, maybe ten years older than I, would visit with me. We raised and trained our own working stock with an occasional trade. Otto and I were soon talking like old friends on the subject.

Mother's sister, Aunt Anna, came to shake hands with me. I had forgotten that she was a much bigger and taller woman than our mother. "Are Grandma and Grandpa resting?" I asked, picturing them lying down in the house. My aunt shook her head. "They just thought the trip would be too hard, Hank," she said. "Your mama's awfully disappointed about it."

"Oh," I said weakly. When would we ever get to see our dear grandparents? Poor Mother, and after she had insisted we talk to them in German.

Pa and Uncle Charles Graphenteen turned from the hogs and my uncle came to shake hands. When I was small I was a little afraid of Aunt Anna's husband. Mother and Uncle Charles sometimes got into really hot arguments, and we children never were sure it was all in fun. I suppose he teased her like a child.

Now Mother came and handed me her milk pail. "You can go wring out Old Iron Teats," she said, referring to a cow. Pa often joked that you had to milk a cow like that and feed the calf, otherwise her calf would starve to death before he could get any milk.

Hilda was herding the little folks toward the house. "I got to get supper," Mother said, and she and the guests followed Hilda. Pa and the other men moved toward our line of horse-drawn machinery, and I went to supervise the last of the evening chores and to milk the hardest milker in the herd.

During supper we heard the latest information on Grandma and Grandpa Lang. They were well but slowing down in activities. Both Ma and Pa had a lot of questions concerning the people and places around Pipestone, Minnesota.

I could barely remember the area, but I did feel homesick for Grandma and Grandpa. All this talk brought back so many memories!

"How are the crops there?" Pa wanted to know. "Had rain? Are they raising corn? I never thought we could grow corn here, so far north, but it's doing good." He turned to Otto and Marie, "Better try to get some land while you're here. Then comes a dry year and you can buy out someone and have a good, big operation!"

The young folks didn't seem very enthusiastic. They no doubt had heard all Uncle Charlie Lang had had to say about Dakota. "You should all come out here," Pa went on. "It's good land, plenty of room for everybody. It isn't such a long trip now or cost so much."

"It's the same distance there," Mother put in.

"Why, you can touch the sun here," Uncle Charles said, "just reach up and touch it." He didn't like the dry, hilly country and he made no secret of it.

Both our parents bragged up the west, while they often had no such kind things to say when we were alone. "I wish the new rooms were done," our pa said between bites of canned pork, fresh garden beans, and boiled potatoes. "It's a good house, but it's too small." I looked around the table on the shady twelve-by-thirty foot east porch where we ate supper in summer time. I was fourteen; Hilda was eleven; Louie, nine; Billy, five; Edward, four; Lester was about two-years-old, and Ella was less than a year. We were a big family for this house!

"I'm so glad to have you come," Mother told her sister, "even if we are a little crowded. Some of the lumber is here, and if we get a crop, we'll have two new bedrooms on the west this fall."

Pa chuckled, "Mamas is always after them old bullsnakes, come sticking their heads up through the holes in the porch floor. She keeps an ax handy just for chasing them. Some say they kill rattlesnakes, but you don't want them in the house. Everybody's building bigger houses now. It's a sign you plan to stay."

Mother tilted her chin up like she always did when she scolded someone. "You don't think it's so funny, you find a snake in your bed one morning! They steal eggs, too, right out of the pail if you leave them set around," she told Aunt Anna. "Sometimes the snakes take eggs from under my setting hens. Some they eat; others you find under some weeds or just out in the yard," she went on.

We began to laugh, picturing Pa finding a bullsnake in his bed. He glared at us and we quieted down quickly. The penalty for bad table manners was a crack on the wrist from Pa's knife handle. No one wanted this to happen with company in the house.

The conversation switched to the soddy, how we had fared there, how the new house was built, and when we had moved in. The ladies had already seen the three rooms, porch, tiny dark pantry, and peeked into the hand-dug cellar. We promised to show the soddy to our guests in the morning. "Yah," Pa sighed, "a soddy would make a good ice house. Most folks use them for a barn or hen house. Ours is part of the barn."

Talk turned to the possibility of keeping ice into the summer. "We are going to try that," Pa declared. He was storing away all the ideas he heard. Pa turned to Mother, "Say, you see if you can get a freezer and make us up some ice cream while they're here," he said.

"And borrow the ice and take it back when we're done with it?" Mother asked. This is typical of her wit. If she hadn't had such a sense of humor, I'm afraid the hardships of life would have been too much for our mother. But she could see the humor in just about anything.

The women talked about who each of us might look like and caught up on more family news. Aunt Anna had never seen the three little boys or Ella. Louie wasn't two when we left Minnesota. We had all changed in size and looks. The folks had written of Christoff's death, but now the sad story had to be told once more along with the one of the fire the day Pa had proved up on the original quarter of land. This seemed a good time to carry some water for my mother, so I left the house.

"It's too bad there aren't trees here," Marie observed as the ladies prepared to do the dishes. It must be hard to haul up enough tree scrap for burning."

"Oh, we're lucky to have the river only a couple miles away," Mother told her. "There's plenty of wood there. The ice knocks down trees and tears them out in flood season. Then they wash up and dry out. We have lots of wood – good cottonwood logs. We use some cow chips in summer, and the boys pick up the corn cobs from the hog yard." Catching her breath, Mother added, "We even have coal! Lignite coal we can dig ourselves, right along the river bank. We can get better coal a few miles east on the Reservation." Was this the same mother who often sounded as though she wished she had stayed in Minnesota or Iowa?

Pa, Louie and I and maybe Billy slept in the barn while our company was there. We had straw ticks, strong cloth ticking filled each fall with new straw. We were haying now, and a tick laid on new hay is a fresh smelling bed indeed. There were goose feather ticks and the good quilts in the house. Mother would see that the company had the best beds.

The young people from Minnesota were "taken up" with sod buildings. Even in the early days of Minnesota, logs had been used if lumber wasn't available. Sod houses were a product of the Dakotas, Nebraska and Kansas where natural groves of trees were few and far apart. We showed our guests where each piece of furniture had stood in the soddy. The two large rooms, one as kitchen and family room and the other with beds all along one wall, wouldn't seem fit to live in. Well it didn't to us now either. That soddy stood and was used as a barn until about 1925.

It must have taken much courage on Mother's part to leave a home with wood floors, curtains on the windows, and a water pump in the yard, and venture with four small children, to live in a two-room soddy the size of a double garage, with dirt floors, earthen walls and the water source a half-mile distant. I wonder if the folks would have made the move had they known what lay in store for the family.

Now that the company had seen the soddy they wanted to hear some pioneer stories. This is one our Pa told: The Grand River, running east, is about two miles south of the homestead. On approaching the river, one finds a high, steep bank called the river bluff. Every so often there is a more gradual slope where with care and good sense, one can get down to the river. In some places it is a fourth-mile or a half-mile to the river itself; in others the river is right down the bank. The flat land along the river is called "river bottom."

The early settlers made it a habit never to travel along the river bottom after dark. People reported seeing yellow lights which bobbed and floated in the air. A man lighted a lantern and hung it on his wagon as he prepared to cross the spooky river bottom.

Some time later he arrived home with shattered nerves and lathered horses. The poor fellow said that the lights had come toward him, and though he whipped up his team to escape, they seemed to be everywhere. Finally a light hit him right in the face. The settler never did fully recover from the shock and fright. This added to everyone's fear of the river area in the dark.

The settlers didn't have scientific explanations for things and often let their superstitions get the best of them. We know there is phosphorus in the soil in some places and that it glows in the dark. The big June bugs might glow if they had hatched in the phosphorus soil. A June bug will follow a light and a big buzzing bug hitting a fellow's face would be frightening.

Another story involves the days before hotels when salesmen and trappers asked to spend the night at farms or ranches along the way. One peddler found himself staying with an old fellow and his son. The evening was spent in silence, but the peddler noticed eight or nine cats under the cook stove or perched on the wood box. The boy seemed deaf or mute or in some way handicapped and the cats were his pets.

At nine o'clock, the old man announced, "Bedtime." The son rose and went to the door. Before he got it opened the father raised his cane and shouted, "Katz!" Cats bounced off the door, the son, the ceiling and each other in a mad scramble for the opening that should have been there! The vision was always good for a laugh.

The stagecoach line from Bismarck, North Dakota, to Pierre, South Dakota, ran south just a few miles east of here, going around the Reservation. It crossed the Grand River at Shooter's Crossing. In the early ranching days the stage ran a couple times a week. There were a couple of kids, about ten-years-old, who had lost their parents to an illness at Bismarck. Somebody put them on the stage for Pierre because they had relatives there. It was late fall, but should have still been safe. Down near Shooter's Crossing they ran into a blizzard. There was no station there and the driver and kids spent an unhappy night in the stagecoach under a bunch of willows. In the morning they went their way and arrived safely.

"I'll tell you some things about the freighters," Pa offered. "Know why they put a rope around the camp?" Most of us didn't know they had. "Well," Pa sat back for a long story. "The freighters brought everything that had come as far as Mobridge by train. The trips here took several days so they camped every night by a creek if they could. That way they could water the horses and wash the dishes." The women shook their heads at that idea. Pa filled his pipe and went on, "They carried all they would need, like drinking water and their food, lantern, bed rolls, oats, all packed in wooden boxes hung along the sides of the freight wagons.

"When we camped at night the men laid a rope on the ground in a circle around the wagon. 'Why the rope?' we asked. We put our bed rolls under the wagon on the ground and everyone crawled into bed. Then the freighters told us that the rope keeps the snakes out of camp. They claimed no one had had a snake in a camp with a rope around it.

"This old fellow called Jake told me how he woke up one time and called his helper. The boy thought there were Indians around, but Jake said no, he had a snake in his pant leg. They both knew if it was a rattlesnake and if it bit Jake, he'd not live long enough to get to a doctor. Jake told the lad to be quiet and get the fire going good and hot. When that was done, Jake told the younger fellow to take a sharp knife and cut the pant leg open. The lad did like he was told, and there was a big ugly rattlesnake trying to keep warm by Jake's leg. They both stayed still, and after a while the rattler started to crawl to the heat and light of the fire. The men killed it then. After that, they always put a rope around the camp."

"You don't keep a cat any more, Carrie," Aunt Anna remarked.

Mother chuckled, "No, but we keep plenty outside. You know I never kept a cat in the house after I caught that one sleeping with the boys when they were little." I had heard many times how I had been almost smothered by the cat. I must have been very little at the time. Sometime the little folks had spilled something under the table and the scambling of cats had been too much for Pa. "No more cats in the house!" he roared, and that was that.

"Once in the soddy we had a rat," Mother was smiling. "I was just finishing the dishes, and Bill was sitting around on the east like he does after supper. Maybe brother Charlie was here, too. I saw the rat run along the ledge on the sod up under the roof, so I hollered quick and Bill came in and grabbed his shotgun and blasted away. The dirt sure flew!" Mother laughed, remembering. "We had a lot of dust for a couple days, and it was a mess to clean up, but no more rat."

"About shooting!" Mother snorted. "There was a stray cat around catching the baby chickens. Louie and Bill cornered him in the barn and Louie moved to head off the cat just as his pa shot. Louie got a pellet in his arm and one just under his eye. Lucky he didn't loose the eye!" Mother had been plenty angry with Pa that time. Louie still carries the pellet, and it never gives him trouble.

Mother put some cow chips into the stove and Aunt Anna said that the burning chips didn't smell as bad as she expected. Mother laughed, "Well, there's better smells!" she said. Then she told the story of Mrs. Wiesinger who had come with her family to a dance. The weather was stormy and they lived quite a ways across the Grand River and south, so the Wiesingers had stayed the night.

In the morning Mother sent a couple of boys to get a tub of chips so she could bake bread. Mrs. Wiesinger told Mother that one of her boys had come into the house one day and remarked,

"Boy, something smells good! Are you baking?" It was the cow chips burning; she hadn't yet begun the baking!

Sunday before our guests left, we had a picnic near the Grand River. Perhaps my parents felt that we should introduce our relatives to the neighbors. It gave us a chance to show off the River, somewhat of a landmark. "The old Indians say there used to be bears along the river," Pa told us. "There's supposed to have been some guy hurt by a bear up where the forks of the river meet. His friends left him for dead. Well, he got on a log and floated down to the Missouri and to some fort and told what happened. They say he was a sight, all scars and sores, flies …"

"Now that's enough!" Mother snapped, knowing how Pa liked to get folks upset with his stories. Today there is a monument to Hugh Glass, who was mauled by a grizzly bear in 1823 near the area where Shadehill is located.

Pa sent Louie on horseback to make arrangements with whoever lived on the place near the river. An Erickson family originally homesteaded there, and later a Backman family, cousins of the Ericksons came, but I can't say when the change took place. The Johnny Sullivans had the farm in the 1940s, and as long as there was school in the neighborhood the picnics were held along the river.

The Ericksons and Backmans stored ice in a cave in the river bank. During floods the ice was thrown up on the banks in chunks the size of stoves and refrigerators. Then folks loaded it up and stored it in straw in a cave. These people made ice cream, much to the pleasure of the neighbor children.

"Be sure to ask if they have ice and if we can use the ice cream freezer," Mother instructed before Louie rode off. "Tell her I'll bring the ice cream makings," she called after him.

My brother returned with a favorable report, so preparations were made. Otto chopped wood for the stove as the ladies baked large sour cream cakes and cooked eggs and potatoes for salad. "The young chicks are too small to fry," Mother decided. So she shut up an old rooster and in the morning Pa killed him. Mother cooled the meat and cooked it for sandwiches. Perhaps the little folks picked lettuce and radishes under Hilda's supervision. There may well have been other good foods; but this was the usual.

Ice cream was made of milk, cream, syrup, eggs and vanilla. Mother poured it into large jars. Everything was packed into the wagon and the buggy, and all but Louie and I climbed in. We rode ahead horseback.

The neighbors had chosen the picnic spot along the river. Now they greeted us warmly. "We had the school picnic here and now company again, how nice!" Everyone smiled and nodded as introductions were made. This was followed by a round of hand shaking among the men and boys.

Ice was put into a burlap bag and chopped with the back of an ax. Then the pieces of ice were packed around the tank or can of liquid ice cream and the lid fitted on. A crank turned a system of gears which in turn operated a paddle that kept stirring the ice cream while it froze.

"I'll turn the crank if the rest of you will eat the ice cream," I announced.

"What? Oh, don't you like ice cream?" "How can you say that?" "I'll eat yours!" "Well, I just love ice cream!" different ones said.

I shook my head and grinned, thinking back to my first and only experience with ice cream. A year or two before, homemade ice cream had been served at a school picnic. "This is the children's day." "Eat up now, you earned it. You all worked so hard." "Like some more there?" The good ladies piled our plates high with picnic foods, and we came back for seconds and thirds of cake, pie and ice cream. I couldn't believe anything could be so delicious! This was cold – colder than fresh well water on a hot day. So sweet and refreshing! I didn't think I would ever get enough of his new treat, ice cream.

But I did! The next day I didn't want to think of food or hear about ice cream. "You'll be ready for lots more next time," Mother said sympathetically. I suspect she knew I was making a pig of myself at the picnic. This time Mother was wrong. I didn't eat ice cream for many years. When it came on the market commercially, I could eat a small helping, but I never liked it a lot.

The picnic was a success whether or not I ate ice cream. After resting in the shade of the cottonwoods for a while, we organized a game of baseball. Rather, we fellows rested while the women  cleared the tables and did dishes. There were no paper plates. We coaxed the girls to join in the ball game. That ended with everyone tired and at least half of us happy, and the mothers were setting out lunch.

"You boys grab a bit quick now and get on home to chores," Pa told us. The sun was getting low as we topped the river bluff and headed north. This day was stored among our happy memories.

Later in the summer of 1915 a frame school house was moved into the district and located a mile south of the farm. This school was named Miller School. I guess because we might have been leasing that quarter of land at the time. It did or still does belong to Henry Kenow. A lot of Millers have attended Miller School. All of the family finished the grades here and eight of the grandchildren attended this school at one time or another. The building still stands, but there hasn't been school since 1948.

It was about this time, 1915, that the schools of the county came under centralized supervision. Texts and programs were standardized and we no longer furnished out own books from the family "library."

The first Perkins County Fair was held in Lemmon in 1915, if I remember right. This summer I was turning fifteen in August; Hilda, twelve in July, and Louie, ten in September. Our Pa took us for one afternoon. We had talked of nothing else for weeks: What is a fair? What does one do and see there? Would we go? And so on.

Once there we stared at the sights and covered our ears against the popping, sputtering gas engines that powered the few rides. Pa looked over the new farm implements and the livestock on display. There may well have been a pulling contest featuring some of the biggest and strongest horses in the area. We probably went to the general store for a few things Mother would have ordered, walked around the fair once more, and went home feeling that the day was a great success.

"Now all the fun and foolishness is over for the year," Pa announced. We children went off to school.

When threshing was done, the men brought loads of lumber to the farm. Pa and the hired man and some of the neighbors went to work on the new and much needed bedrooms. The foundation was poured for the rooms along the west side of the house. I missed school to help with sawing and nailing. As the days grew shorter and cooler, Louie, too, spent days at home helping with the building.

Finally the west windows of the kitchen and living room were removed and the spaces cut into doors. The windows were set into the new outside walls. The rooms could be heated with the rest of the house and work went on inside. We boys got to school more regularly.

It must have been a great treat to our mother to have a three-bedroom home for her family. We hoped to get a porch or entry built to fill out the southwest corner, but that had to wait until spring. The entry, when it materialized, was known as "the shed." It did help keep mud, flies and cats out of the house as well as covering the kitchen door against the hot sun.

This was likely the summer that our Pa felt prosperous enough to afford a corn binder. This machine worked much like the grain binder; it cut and tied bundles of corn. The corn binder had two tongues and three horses were used to power it. It took strong arms and backs to put up corn shocks. Late in the fall, we hauled in the heavy shocks, picked out the ears of corn for the hogs, and fed the stalks and leaves to the cows. It wasn't silage, but it was feed.

Something I remember about hauling corn shocks is one hired man who would go and work bare handed. We were surprised to see him go without gloves or mitts. Pa offered him some, thinking he didn't own any. "Oh, no thanks. I don't need any unless I handle iron," he said pleasantly. I shivered and banged my cold hands while he grinned and pitched corn without any mitts! He just didn't seem to get cold.

-15-
END OF SCHOOL DAYS FOR ME

The spring of 1916, I think, we began cutting our own ice from the Grand River. I stayed out of school to help. Later I went back to finish my seventh grade and got my diploma after tests that spring. I still have the diploma. I was fifteen and one-half, and beginning to feel that I had outgrown school. I could read anything I picked up, and I wasn't learning anything new at school.

Pa had decided he had to learn to read, or maybe read better. By using our books and asking questions, he learned to read English. I felt I could do as well.

Pa remained an eager student of newspapers and farm magazines as long as his sight would permit reading. He read the German and later the English papers from Pipestone, Minnesota, and the Lemmon paper or papers and several magazines. After retirement our dad read as much as three or four hours a day.

In the spring of 1916, Donald joined the family. Hilda stayed home from school to look after the little children and do the cooking and dishes. One evening she told us that the lady who came that day had put the baby's thumb into his mouth before she had gone home. "As soon as she was gone, Ma said,

'Take it out quick, 'fore he finds out he likes it,'" our sister said. I doubt that any of us developed the habit of thumb sucking!

Our three little brothers, Billy, Edward, and Lester ranged along about ten years younger than I. Those who are not kept busy find something to do, and they were good at it! I especially remember one day I walked in from a field to find the three of them playing with wood blocks in the water tank. Feet and rears waving, and bodies off balance, the boys leaned over the edge of the large stock tank – full of water.

How many times our parents had warned them that one might fall in and drown! *I should paddle all of you,* I thought. I sneaked up and grabbed the nearest one by the seat of his pants and upset his balance. Eddy's head went under water, and I jerked him up as though to rescue him.

"Oh, my! Did you fall in? Well, Eddy, Mama's been saying that might happen, hasn't she?"

How Edward howled when he got his breath! Billy, the oldest, looked like he suspected I may have had something to do with the "accident." No small brother let me catch him hanging over the edge of the water tank after that.

I was about sixteen and Hilda, thirteen, when we began going to dances and parties without our parents. We took a team and buggy and we went and came home together for several years. Sometimes we rode horseback, but that is a little unhandy for a young lady. Some folks frowned on girls riding, but Hilda liked to ride, and she was a good rider. Often she wore a pair of my jeans and took her skirt in a cloth bag, then changed in the outhouse before going in to the party.

These were barn dances, more of a public dance than the house parties we had known as little children. These were attended by older teens and the young married folks, although some brought families.

The story is told of a large family who were nearly home when the father asked one boy a question. Getting no reply, he began checking his load and found that he was short a boy. It seems that they had quite a long trip back for the missing youngster. After that the father called "roll" before leaving for home.

Pa always had a hard job planned for the day after a dance or party and he would call us extra early. Maybe it was a private joke with him, or perhaps he was telling us that if fun interferes with work it is time to cut down on the fun.

After harvest in 1916, I went back to school for a few weeks but I had lost interest and I felt out-of-place. I knew my folks could use my help at home, so I just quit going to school and no one seemed to care one way or the other. Later I heard a joke about being kicked out of school. After that if someone asked why I wasn't at school, I said I'd been kicked out in the second grade because I wouldn't shave.

The frame school was the center of the community just as the sod one had been. There was a Christmas party or little program just before vacation began. This was likely an afternoon thing and I found an excuse not to go this time. We men were too busy to go to the end-of-the-year party. But we wouldn't miss the Sunday picnic. My, they were fussy now with the county in charge of the schools. They were going to have school until May! It had always ended in April, depending a little on the weather and on whether the teacher was a farmer.

-16-
GROWING UP

In late summer of 1917, Marie wrote that Grandma Lang was ill and that the doctor had been called. The illness was considered serious. "That settles it!" Mother said firmly, "I've just got to get back and see my mother before it's too late. Do I go on the train or shall I borrow a mule to ride?" She must have expected some argument.

"You and Hilda both go. Take the baby. Ella can round us up something to eat and do the dishes," Pa said generously. Don was about a year-and-a-half old and Ella somewhat past three. Our mother made plans to take them both. She and Hilda did extra baking and got the laundry and mending all caught up for us along with all their regular work and the packing. Pa drove Mother, Hilda, Ella and baby Don to meet the train in Lemmon a few days later. I hoped that some other time I might see my grandparents.

While Mother and our sisters were away, Pa decided he would make the gravy one evening as we "rounded up" some boiled potatoes and fried pork to go with bread, milk and cake. After frying the meat, Pa put it on the plate as he had seen Mother do. Then he took the flour sifter, which held four or more cups, and shook flour into the pan of fat on the stove. "We want plenty of gravy," he said, and he shook in another cup of flour.

Well! He got plenty of gravy! The mixture got terribly thick and gooey, so Pa added more milk and more and more. He kept thinning the gravy and soon had a kettle full or more and none of it any good. At this point, our Pa decided to bake the concoction. He filled Mother's big bread pan with gravy and put it into the oven. The large flat pans held four or five loaves of bread and had handles at each end. "We'll just cut this like corn bread," Pa promised.

The gravy had no yeast or other leavening in it, so it baked hard as a brick. Pa cussed and threw it out, and then he was angry with the dog because he wouldn't eat the "gravy." In a day or so the smaller boys gathered up the chunks and gave them to the hogs.

I took over in the kitchen and have always enjoyed doing a bit of cooking. Mother came home happy and refreshed. Grandma was better and everyone expected her to recover. She did, and lived several years. I got to know the little folks better and learned to appreciate my mother's work and problems by helping her that winter.

I took over the care of the hens, and I planned to keep them laying all winter.

"Ha," Pa scoffed. "Hens ain't supposed to lay in winter."

"They will if they have good care, a warm place and warm water to drink," I countered. The farm paper said so, and I was going to try.

"If you can get them laying again by Easter we'll have an egg eating contest," Mother promised. "I'll cook up the eggs, and we'll see just who can eat the most."

I carried warm water to the hens twice a day all winter. I fixed the feeders up off the ground so the birds might keep their feet warm. I patched up the hen coop and did my best to pamper the chickens and keep them comfortable. The hens laid eggs for us all winter! Not a lot, but enough for baking and pancakes and Sunday morning egg gravy sometimes.

Egg gravy is a sort of thickened egg nog done in a fry pan and spooned over toast for breakfast. This was a Sunday morning treat for years.

This winter or the next one, some of us older boys rode horseback to the "badlands," rough country south the Grand River. We chose and cut some of the little evergreen trees that clung to the steep slopes there. For the first time in many years we had a green Christmas tree. And for years after that, our tree came home on horseback or at the end of a lasso from the Grand River breaks.

Decorations were still cut from the pretty sides of magazine or catalogue pages; maybe we had popcorn and wild berries to string, too. I have mentioned the school party or program. Some years we may have gone to church, but most often not. It was a long trip and often too cold for such a ride.

Easter was the time for the family egg eating contest. Again, I doubt if we got to church, depending on how early it fell and the weather and work. It was important that the confirmation class members go, but Sunday morning was a different story.

Birthdays at home were usually celebrated with a plain cake. None of us ever had birthday parties as children. Mother most often managed to have something for us, a shirt or dress or a pair of socks or mittens. When we got to earning a little, we could get a little something for our parents' birthdays, too.

-17-
WAR!

Every time Pa went to town during the winter and spring of 1918 he came home upset. "All the Old Country's going to war," he'd say. Our Pa had talked with some who read newspapers sent in from Chicago, Illinois, and Minneapolis, Minnesota. The war had held little interest for us until Germany became involved in 1914, and then Pa worried about his relatives. Many of the German people in the area were quietly cheering for their fatherland. The United States entered World War I in the spring of 1917 when I was sixteen-and-a-half. Even this did not affect us much except that there was a little more demand for food grains and meat.

There were times when we couldn't get wheat flour and the women had to bake with barley flour. That was sticky and not very good. It was a poor joke that the folks who raised the wheat had to settle for barley flour. In the early poor years, we had sometimes soaked whole wheat overnight and used the cooked grain as cereal, but this was different. We raised the wheat, could afford the flour, and couldn't get it.

Some folks criticized the United States President for getting us into the war while others thought he should have done it sooner. We heard that eighteen-year-olds would have to register for the draft. After a while even the German-Americans were angry about the bombing of neutral ships. Many wouldn't admit to being German any more.

The spring of 1918, Pa came from town one day in a great rage. He unhitched his team, slapped the animals with the lines, and sent them to the barn where I was at work. Thinking that something must be very wrong, I quickly tied the horses and ran to the house. I came in to hear Pa say, "Carrie, I got cousins there, nephews! How can I send my boy to shoot at them?"

Mother was crying. "Maybe it'll be over by then, Bill. This register, it don't mean go, does it?"

"I hope not! Mein Gott, this makes a man old!" Pa stormed.

I stepped in and slammed the door so they'd know they weren't alone. "You got to register for their rotten war, boy," Pa said, sort of shaky. Mother dried her eyes.

"I know, but not 'til I'm eighteen, and that's three months yet," I tried to sound cheerful.

Pa told us how he had seen the train leave Lemmon and on it some of the first of the local boys to go the training camps. It had upset him so, and now all of us. The war hung over us like a plague from then on. When I turned eighteen in August, I was down with the flu. The neighbors Wagner brought the mail when they came from town. In there was a letter saying I should come in to register.

Pa saddled a horse and rode into Lemmon to see if I had to come right away. He returned to report that I must wait until I was thoroughly over the flu. This was the terrible flu of 1918 when so many people died. Somehow all of our family survived. A little neighbor boy was lost and several others not as close neighbors as the Hoeflings lost dear ones.

Feelings ran high on the war subject while I took my time in getting well. One lady said she'd rather shoot her boy herself than send him to fight his relatives. Folks were in a general uproar over the whole business. When I did go to register I was asked a lot of questions about the family, how large the farm and if my parents were well.

Just as Mother hoped, the war ended in November of 1918, so I never found out what kind of a soldier I'd have made. Hard as it was losing Christoff, I think it would have been worse had he gone and been lost in Europe. Being a year older than I, he would almost surely have been among the first to go, especially with two older boys and so many younger ones to help at home.

Both Louie and I had to register for World War II, but we had families and were too old for soldiering by that time. Our younger brothers, Lester and Billy, both spent several years serving our country. Les was in Alaska and Bill in Europe and Africa in some of the worst fighting. Our parents aged a lot from worrying about the boys, but they perked up when the soldiers were safe at home.

By 1918 the Perkins County Fair was a regular two-day event. Our Pa and Mr. Hoefling, among others, worked as extra policemen during the fair. The whole family would go. Often we took two outfits, say a wagon and the buggy. Some would go home to do chores and put the little tots to bed while the rest took in the evening midway, stage show or whatever. Then turn about the next night.

There was a Ferris wheel, loud music and sometimes a merry-go-round. Pa would say, "Hah? Pay money to ride that when we got thirty horses to home?" We did ride the Ferris wheel, those of us who had the courage, and we shot darts for prizes we probably didn't win. The boys watched the girls, and the girls talked about boys; some things don't change. The local sheriff closed some of the fair booths for cheating the public. Seems there was a selection of strings to pull for a prize. But none were tied to any good prizes.

One time I had a job selling hamburgers at the fair. A woman did the cooking, but I enjoyed shouting the wares and making change. This was likely one of my first jobs other than helping other farmers when our dad traded work with a neighbor.

The Indians came with their wagons, set up the cone-shaped teepees and stayed for the whole fair. Horses were hobbled or picketed along roads or in grassy areas, cook fires built, and an old fashioned Indian village became real before our curious stares. Most came for the rodeo, and many were winners. Even into the 1940s the Indians came and camped. Not many had cars until after the war when many used cars came on the market.

Most boys over ten years of age had a pocket knife. When I was about seventeen or eighteen, a new game showed up. At a dance or in town, someone would step up and say, "How'd ya like to trade knives?" The trade was sight unseen to make it more fun. If you didn't trade, you were looked down on, and if you did, you may lose a good knife and get a rusty old relic with no blades. We soon learned to leave good knives at home and carry a junker. I lost a couple good knives, and I got rid of several worthless ones before the game wore itself out.

-18-
BIG FAMILY, BIG FARM

In the late teens or early 1920s, the steam tractors came on the farm scene. This was something our pa decided we must have. "Look how much faster we can plow!" he pointed out. So Pa went to the bank and got a loan to buy a tractor. Apparently he didn't have any trouble getting the money. He did have a pet theory concerning bankers; that one pay the banker first, then if need be, borrow again and pay others. That isn't original, but he seemed to think so, and it kept him on good terms at the bank.

The first tractor was a Grey. The Grey was a monster on steel wheels as high as a man's head. It clanked and growled, burned wood or straw, smoked and smelled, moved slower than the slowest horse. But it could pull a big plow, and we felt like big farmers. The big plows had eight or ten bottoms and were more long than wide. There was a plank across the front, and man walked along this to set the levers. As the tractor moved into the field, each bottom in turn had to be lowered. The tractor moved slowly enough so that wasn't much of a strain. But you did have to watch what you were doing. At the end of the furrow, the plow man lifted all the bottoms out again.

Many stories are now being told about steam engines because of renewed interest in antique machinery. Getting stuck in the mud with a tractor and plow was quite something. Some chose to gather as many horses as necessary along with block and tackle for whatever leverage it gave and pull the huge tractor out. Others just threw up their hands and left the machinery stand there until the mud dried up and the tractor could be heated up and driven out. This was by far the easiest and least exciting.

With a big family of boys and a hard-working wife to help, Pa built from four horses and four cows in a sod barn on a quarter section, to ten quarters of his own plus ten or so that he leased or rented from time to time. All this wasn't farm land, a good share was pasture and hayland. It takes a lot of ground to support a cow or a big horse in this area.

About now the telephone lines were brought to our neighborhood. I was home only part of the time, but I know my mother especially enjoyed the phone. What a treat to be able to talk to a neighbor or to call into town! The phone had been installed at standard height so Mother needed a little stool to stand on so she could reach the mouthpiece. All her life, she called, "Hullo?" as though she was talking to someone far away when she used the phone.

On the country lines there were several parties, all of whom could hear each other's telephone ring. One party answered to a long ring, another to a short ring, someone else to two shorts and so on. I believe one long meant trouble and everyone listened in to see if they could help. The party doing the calling turned a crank to produce the ringing, so they were never quite all the same. And the curious and not-too-busy soon learned to listen in or "rubber" when others talked on the phone.

One neighbor had a loud ticking clock, and when she listened to her neighbors, they could hear that clock. I was told by Pa and the amused youngsters that one day Mother wasn't just her usual cheerful self and on hearing that clock, she snapped, "Hang up the phone, Mrs. _____. I know you're there. I can hear your clock!" I have an idea that "Mrs." covered the mouthpiece thereafter, but I doubt if she stopped rubbering.

The neighbors, the Erlenbusch family, invited us to have Thanksgiving dinner with them in 1919. As it turned out, our mother had to spend the day in bed. Edna was born that morning. Our mother insisted that we young folks go, as the neighbors were planning on us. Hilda fixed something for our folks to eat, and we went out to dinner. We told the family when we got to Erlenbusch's that we had a new baby sister.

"Did you hear about the 'turkey' that came to Millers this morning?" Mrs. Erlenbusch said to the others who came. So Edna became our little "Thanksgiving turkey."

We were a family of 10 with a big house as well as the bunk house. I expect some of us older members were more or less on our own. The whole season of Thanksgiving through New Year was quite happy for all.

-19-
MEN'S WORK

Most young fellows worked the roads at some time or another, and quite a few of the established farmers did, too. After the crops were planted in 1920, Louie and I went to work on what is now Highway 73 running south toward Bison. Later in the summer, we moved with the contractor over to what is now U.S. Highway 212 near Faith, South Dakota. By putting on teams, this meant using our own horses, we made what was then very good pay. Louie was just fifteen that summer, but he was so tall no one asked his age, and he could hold a man's place in the working world.

The digging work was done with a sort of a big shovel called a Fresno. This implement was pulled by four horses, and the driver walked behind holding a long handle and guiding the scoop as well as the horses. We drove into the earth to be moved, scooped up a bucketful and holding onto the handle, drove to the roadbed where we dumped the earth. In dumping, the Fresno handle flew high in the air, then was jerked back by a long rope toward the driver before it tipped clear over onto the horses. Great care and good timing were needed to avoid getting banged on the head by the iron handle when it came down. Other tools, rollers, and packers were used to spread and level the new roadbed.

It wasn't long until the boss asked me to try the water wagon. This meant pumping a tank of water from a river or stream and hauling it to the grade where it was sprinkled onto the road as the packing was done. There may have been more than one water wagon depending on the distance we were hauling.

Many horses were not suited to the water wagon because it is necessary to back the wagon into the creek for filling. Most horses will give a pull, and if the load doesn't come, they become upset and begin jumping and jerking. The water wagon team had to slowly lean into their collars (part of the harnesses) and keep steady pressure until the load began to move.

Sometimes this took a minute or more, but my horses just kept leaning, and the mud around the wheels would begin to gurgle, and the wheels would begin to move. I was using a great big team of Pa's, and they were good ones. He probably sent some of the best with us. I was proud of the way we could take on a load like that and handle it! Later I bought the team.

The contractor provided a cook tent where we ate and a bunk tent where we slept on cots. He provided hay and feed for working stock. Three or four men were hired to do the cooking and dishes for the workmen. It was a general rule that anyone who grumbled about the menu could spend the next meal or two working in the cook tent. The cooks were very touchy about it if anyone even might be criticizing the food, and several workers got the "cook tent cure."

One morning we sat at the long table in the center of the tent and the cooks began setting out plates piled high with pancakes. A few guys began to grin and others shook their heads. The pancakes were the fattest, doughiest I ever saw, and we wondered who would be first to say something about that. We began eating. The cakes were the worst I've ever put a fork to!

One of the boys threw down his fork and burst out, "These are the awfu–u–best pancakes I ever et!" The place rocked with shouts of laughter. How near the lad had come to earning a turn in the cook tent!

Another time we had rice for dinner, rice for supper, and more rice the next day. Then word leaked out that the cooks had a recipe calling for 3/4 cup of rice. They had read it as "three or four" cups and then multiplied that to feed thirty or more men. The poor fellows had every container in the place filled with swelling rice!

Most of the time the cooks did a good job. It is not easy to cook for so many and to do it practically outdoors. The cook stove sat at the end of the tent with a pipe running up. If it was rainy or windy the men put up a tent fly to protect themselves. Otherwise the tent was open at the ends to let the air pass through. It was hot in the summer and chilly late in the fall and generally unhandy.

Our boss was an Irishman about sixty, but he was very active and energetic. He had some mules of his own on the machinery, and the men who drove them were responsible for their care. Many of the guys had trouble with the mules, but the boss could make them work. He used a big whip and some terrible language. We were never sure which helped the most.

Anyone who would not try driving the mules was considered a sissy, so most everyone gave them a try. I got along, but I like to have a friendly time with my animals and a mule more or less has to be forced to do his share. With them you can't relax; you never know what is going to happen. I never liked the brutes.

One Sunday afternoon, the road workers were sitting around visiting, playing cards or napping when a couple of cars chugged up to the camp. We watched, but no one moved. Then our Pa's voice rang out, "Any Millers here?" he hollered. We jumped right up and hiked over to the cars.

"You know these folks?" Pa asked. Well, it was my cousin, Marie, her husband, Otto Schuldt, her sister, Rose, and Rose's husband, Art, whom we had never met. There was a little girl about seven whom I'd never seen. She and Ella were pretty chummy, and it turned out she was Aunt Anna's youngest, Elsie. Mother and Aunt Anna and Uncle Charles Graphenteen filled out the loads. Marie's kids and Rose's, if she had any, had stayed at the farm with Hilda.

The fellows moved around to admire the dusty cars, and the family moved into the shade of trees or tents to visit. Uncle Charles said it was even hotter and drier here than at the farm. He may well have been right, and I suspect that he and Mother were still arguing the point.

We heard news of the rest of the family – Grandma and Grandpa Lang and the little aunts, Mary and Tina. I realized that if I was almost grown so must they be. I tried not to think of them as little girls any more. "It would mean so much to the folks to see Carrie and the children," Aunt Anna said.

"I always hope to get back," Mother sighed. "The time goes so fast and always a baby. I guess Hank and Hilda could take care of things if we ever have the money for the trip."

"I guess so," Pa said. "How far is it? Does it cost so much?" he asked. Maybe this fall or winter, Ma and I could take the train, I thought. That was a good idea. I'd save more of my pay after this. We had to give Pa a share, probably half, for the use of the teams. The contractor wouldn't pay us all we had coming until quitting time in the fall. Even then, there would be enough for trip and my winter expenses.

The young people said Hilda had taken them over to see the abandoned sod school, but it was badly tumbled down. Then they drove to the frame school. I was pleased that the company had been "shown around." Pa explained, likely for the second or third time, that wind, frost and snow ruin a soddy if it isn't regularly repaired. Then he told us that several had slept in the old soddy part of the barn so they could say they'd slept in a soddy. Little Elsie had gotten scared and moved back to the house. I didn't blame her a bit; there were always mice and often rats out there.

The little girls were taken up with us "cowboys" and the big hats we all wore. We got hold of the smallest, gentlest horse in camp, loaned them some hats and gave them a ride. In later years, Elsie recalled that we went somewhere and picked berries and she and Ella ran ahead and came upon a rattlesnake.

They were some mighty scared little girls. Someone killed the snake, and the trip was a success.

"Hank, aren't you worried? Louie's catching up to you." Aunt Anna had to tease us a little. We grinned; I was twenty or very close to it and Louie was fifteen, and he'd been over my head for two years.

"He takes after Papa and Charlie," Mother put in. I thought of how big Uncle Charlie Lang was, at least in a boy's memory. I could hardly remember Grandpa Lang, but it is said he was a big man.

I glanced at the cars. How proud and sturdy they were! Would Pa ever buy one? When would I have one of my own? I suspect that we all thought that Rose and Marie had married well-to-do men, which they may have.

One of the young men asked if there were any "real" cowboys in the area. There were, especially north and west of Lemmon where Ed "Dad" Lemmon, the founder of the town, had set up his large cattle operation in the 1880s. And there was the Lyman spread south of the Grand River and ranging eastward.

"Let me tell you a cowboy story," Pa chuckled. "There was a bunch of Lyman's men in town one night really whooping it up. After while it got too tame – or the marshal asked them to leave. They rode out toward the ranch. Not many carry hand guns, but they do. Well, this was a few years back." Pa paused a bit, then went on, "They were shooting in the air and hollering and racing the horses. After things quieted down a bit, one guy let go with another pistol shot. His horse had just had enough of this foolishness and began bucking. The lad was a little tipsy and sleepy anyway, he let the gun get to bouncing and the next shot got the horse in the neck. Killed it right there!"

"Uncle Bill, is that a true story?" Marie asked in distress. Pa assured her that it was, and had happened only a couple miles south and east of home. It would have been a cowboy's best, or his best looking horse that he would have taken into town, too.

Pa was in a story telling mood. "You know when Mr. Lemmon first came out here there weren't many settlers, and his ranch hands were all like a big family. So the boys got to calling him "Dad" and now he's "Dad Lemmon" to the whole country side. They say once one of his boys, his ranch hand, wanted to borrow ahead on his pay. The lad asked if he might have a loan of five dollars. Mr. Lemmon put his hand behind his ear, 'Eh?' he asked."

"Loan me five bucks?" the lad repeated.

Again Mr. Lemmon indicated that he had not heard. "Can I have ten dollars?" the cowhand said loudly.

"I heard you the first time," Mr. Lemmon said as he handed him the five dollars.

Aunt Anna's sons-in-law had figured gallons of gasoline, miles and cost of the trip. "Well, we ain't got a car anyway," Pa said gruffly.

"There's always the train," Aunt Anna reminded him. She looked over at Rose, "It might be safer than driving, too." Our guests were laughing and looking at my cousin, Rose.

"Yah, Rosie got sea-sick on the ferry at Mobridge," Uncle Charles told us.

"It's a long way across that old river, and the ferry rocked and swayed so," Rose said.

"That's all right, let them laugh. It can happen to anybody," Mother said sympathetically. "The river's higher than usual; they say there's been lots of rain farther north and west."

"That wasn't so bad, but we ran into a sand storm not ten miles beyond the river," one of the young men said.

"Sea-sick and sand storm!" Pa laughed.

"Oh, it was awful!" Aunt Anna insisted, "So dark and sand blowing into your teeth and hair!"

"We were lost, and the kids bawled," Marie told us. "The road's just an old wagon trail this side of the river."

"I suppose so," our pa said then. "That's the Indian Reservation, and no one will build them a road until someone else needs one there. You're lucky it didn't rain, or you'd still be there."

"We did have to stay in a little town until the wind went down," someone else said.

"If I ever come again, I'll come on the train," Aunt Anna informed us.

"Me, too," others agreed.

"Never again! No more of this country for me!" our uncle declared. "I don't know why folks live here – hot, dry, windy."

"Well, I'm sure sorry," Mother snapped. "The wind does blow a lot. We get used to it, I guess. Seems there's been an extra lot of it lately," she added pointedly.

"A four-horse team couldn't drag me out here again," our uncle said.

Pa was getting "hot under the collar." "I'll not be lending anyone the horses to try it, either," he retorted. I'm still not sure that was all in fun.

Along in the afternoon, the young men spun the cranks and the Model T cars sputtered to life. Noise and smoke poured forth. The car loads of passengers lurched out of camp and turned north. We called, "Goodbye." "Good luck." "Write when you get home," and such polite things, but we were a little stung at how our home country looked to some of the relation.

I hope our company enjoyed their visit to South Dakota because it was the last trip most of them made. Folks get older and young families grow larger; work and responsibilities take more time, and somehow no one made the trip again for many years.

Mother's second brother, John Lang, did visit in about 1936, and Aunt Mary, who became Mrs. Reedy, stopped at Lemmon several times on her way from Minnesota to California in more recent years. I last saw her in 1957 when she could still travel by train. Tina moved to Canada, and I have lost track of her. All of the aunts and uncles and Rose and Art and Otto are gone. Marie lives in Pipestone, Minnesota, and Elsie is Mrs. Everett Hatfield. They live at Ortonville, Minnesota.

Most years the ground freezes earlier, but that year we worked until late fall. Sleeping on a canvas cot in a tent in October is next to impossible, we found. One evening some of the older hands came carrying armloads and forkfuls of hay into the tent. They peeled the bedding from their cots, spread the hay on the canvas, replaced the blankets, and advised us to do the same. After that we got a lot more sleep on chilly nights.

We worked on the road until just before Thanksgiving. When we got home we were saddened to learn of Grandma Lang's passing. The telegram had been phoned out to the farm a few weeks before.

Our parents had put Hilda in charge at home and both took the train to Pipestone to attend services. They spent a week or so with the family there. Grandma's death was a blow to me as I had still hoped to see her again. Since I wouldn't be traveling to Minnesota, I dickered with Pa and used the money to buy the big horses I had driven all summer.

The youngsters were still talking cars at home. Everyone had been treated to a car ride during the summer, and we thought having an auto would be just the thing. "You want a car we can't even use in winter or some new shoes and coats?" Pa finally asked gruffly. "We can't have both. There's things we need. A car we been getting along fine without. Look at all the trouble people have with the things." We knew he was right, but that didn't stop boys from dreaming and talking cars when Pa wasn't around. When we did get a "motor" it was a truck, and a year or two passed before Pa bought a car.

After Thanksgiving, Louie went back to school to pick up the few credits he needed to finish the eighth grade.

In late winter or early spring of 1921, Grandpa Lang passed away. None of our family went to Pipestone this time. There was no one now who needed their comforting presence, and our mother didn't feel up to making the trip again.

Once the crops were in for 1921, Louie and I took teams and a wagon and journeyed to near Mobridge where a crew was beginning construction on what is now old US Highway 12.

Travel between Lemmon and Mobridge, South Dakota, and you can still see where we built the road around the hills in several places. About five miles west of McIntosh, you can see the old road going north around a hill, and on the other side it curves back to almost meet the new road. All this has been redone at least once. This piece of Highway 12 was the last to be hard-surfaced. It was a dusty gravel road into the 1950s while all the rest was tarred coast to coast.

This job was a little different in that we had to camp and sleep in our wagon – or under it as we chose. We had to take turns horse wrangling. Every so often, two fellows would herd the working stock as they grazed in the night, then the boys would have the next day off.

At the time there was no bridge for the highway, only the railroad bridge or the ferry if we needed to get across the Missouri River. We walked across the railroad bridge often, as there was a charge for using the ferry.

Late one day, after the night herd boys had gotten their sleep, they decided to go into Mobridge. They started across the bridge as we had all done many times. The boys were part-way across when a train came roaring out of the west hills. Knowing they couldn't outrun the train, the fellows stood on the sides of the tracks and held onto the platform where some water barrels were mounted. The water was for putting out fires if the train threw sparks onto the wooden bridge.

The boys held onto the water barrels or lay clinging to the ties as the train roared past nearly shaking them off the bridge. This must have been enough excitement, as the hikers then headed back for camp on the west side. Before they were off the bridge a train came from the east and nearly caught up to them. The lads hadn't paid any attention, thinking the noise was the east-bound getting into town. Shortly before it was too late, the boys ducked under the bridge and hung onto the braces while the train steamed by overhead. They came out pale and sick and nearly deaf, but suffered no permanent problems.

Imagine the kidding I got when we came in from the day's work to hear what my "little" brother had been doing on his day off! We didn't fiddle along on the bridge after that, but hustled right across. We watched for trains a lot more carefully, too. The road bridge was built south of the railroad span in 1924. Both are gone now and new high bridges a mile long cross the Missouri farther north and accommodate the Missouri River Lakes.

In the fall of 1921, Dad come out to the road crew and Louie returned to the farm. The task of harvesting the fields by hand-picking the corn fell to Louie, Billy, Les, and Edward. A freak farm accident claimed Edward's life while Dad and I were away.

-20-
GROWN UP
1922-26

I was furious with my pa when I came home from road work the fall of 1922 and found my littlest brother limping around on a leg he had injured early in the summer. Don had slipped off the low cement step at the back door and, Pa had proclaimed, "Such a little fall couldn't hurt a boy very much." But it had, and the leg hadn't been set. A father's word was law, but I believe if I'd been home, I'd have taken the boy to a doctor. By the time a doctor saw the leg, it had healed wrong.

Don has had no end of trouble with that leg. He has always been the most pleasant and cheerful person in spite of that. Clara, who would later marry my brother, Louie, was Don's first teacher and she has told us how he would sit and cry while others played at recess.

Our pa's teeth hurt him for years, and he was often gruff and short for that reason. He got dentures and they weren't much better. Pa would get the dentures overloaded at meal time, then plop the whole mess onto the table and eat toothless. This got to be too much! One day I stood up and told him he had no business leaving that there for us all to see and several other things that had been grating at me. After that, we were on a man-to-man basis, not as man and boy. He was a lot more careful about the dentures, too.

About this time we older boys got to calling him "Dad" rather than "Pa" or "Papa" and the younger children followed. Mother always called our dad "Pa." We called her "Ma" or "Mother" except for the younger sisters who went modern and said "Mom." Dad always called our mother his pet name, "Mamas." Maybe that simply meant more than one mama, and busy as she often was, it fit.

A young man's wages were expected to help out with the family until he was of age, that is twenty-one. We did use Dad's horses the first year or two that we did road work. Both Louie and I bought our first teams from Dad during this time. That was the beginning of anyone's farm.

I got my first car when some used ones came onto the market, but that is another story. I remember a truck our dad had gotten about now. At the time the school teacher often boarded with one family then another, perhaps a month at a time. On one occasion Louie and I "just happened" to be going by the young lady's home and would give her a ride home for the weekend. The old trucks had narrow cabs and a floor shift. Before long I noticed that Louie was "having" to shift for every little knoll and the poor girl was having a terrible time keeping her knees out of his way!

The first winter I had my own team, we were hauling grain into Lemmon and bringing out coal for us and the school. There was a lot of snow in the range of hills north, so we hauled south to the Grand River, went west on the ice, then north into Lemmon on what is now Highway 73. Les and Bill were the young helpers on the day I recall.

Our dad was in a hurry to get started, but I had decided to shoe my horses first. "Aw, you waste time!" he scoffed. I went ahead and prepared to cold shoe my team. We had shoes that fit most of the horses, and we just tacked them on if we planned to be on ice or gravel. Horses can get sore feet awfully fast on the gravel, but we didn't use shoes for field work. I began shoeing my horses, and Dad growled, "If you're gonna fool around at that, I may as well shoe mine while I wait." So he shod his horses just on the front feet, then he left with his load. I shod my team on the back feet as well. This takes a little longer, as most horses are a little fussier about their hind feet. I tried to keep my horses used to having their feet handled, and now was when those extra few minutes and kind words paid off.

Eventually Les and I left with our load. Before we'd gone five miles, we caught up with Dad. His horses were skidding and slipping on the ice and having a dreadful time pulling the loaded bobsled. We waved and hallowed as we passed. At the point where we left the river, we waited for them for quite a while. I couldn't help feeling a little cocky, although a lad shouldn't. It was so hard for our dad to believe that we boys knew anything. I had to enjoy the incident.

Before we left for home, Dad stopped at the blacksmith shop and had his team shod on both their front and back feet. With four spikes on each foot, the horses had no trouble in getting the loads home in good time.

In 1923, our dad bought an old threshing machine and we did custom work around the community. We had the steam engine to power the machine and lots of boys and horses. We almost made up a crew by ourselves. This was a more modern thresher of grey sheet metal on the outside, and more durable than the wooden, horse-powered ones of the earlier years. The steam engine turned the works by means of a long fiber belt that ran from the huge pulley wheel on the engine to a pulley on the thresher. This machine ran fast enough for a fan to blow straw through a long pipe into a gleaming, golden pile. This straw was often hauled back to be burned in the steamer. An elevator carried the threshed grain up to a spout and poured it into a wagon.

The header was used for cutting grain when the straw was short. Horses were hitched to a pole that pushed the machine. The driver stood on a platform behind the teams and steered the header with a "pilot pole." A wide lugged wheel carried the main weight of the machine and powered the sickle, reel, canvas, and elevator by chains and sprockets. A sickle in front cut the grain onto a canvas that carried it up an elevator to a header box on a wagon pulled alongside by another team. The box was an unusual looking piece of equipment, high on one side and low on the other. Headings were sometimes stacked to be threshed later and other times pitched directly into the thresher.

When the binder was used, men and boys hauled bundles and pitched them onto a conveyer belt that carried them into the bowels of the thresher. Someone else hauled water in a tank on a wagon and kept the steam engine supplied with water for boiling into steam. That wagon was on the go all the time, making trips from a creek or farm well to the thresher.

How many men and boys made a crew? Well, an engineer who managed the tractor and machine, a boy to help feed the engine, two on the water wagon, eight or ten to haul bundles, one or two to haul away and shovel grain into bins made up a working crew. If a couple more boys could stay out of school so much the better.

We must not forget the ladies who fixed huge and good meals for the menfolk. Many did this cooking themselves, while some had their own girls or hired one for fifty cents a day during threshing. Once we were at some peoples' home and saw some most unusual coffee. The lady poured her husband's coffee first, and it was thick as syrup. I couldn't believe anyone could drink it, but he did. Then the woman poured a couple gallons of hot water into the big coffee pot she had, and the rest of us drank that coffee. It was good.

Later in the fall we picked corn by hand and tossed the husked ears into the wagon box as the team stood waiting. Louie and I often picked on opposite sides of the wagon, and after a while we'd get bored. For a bit of fun, we'd toss an ear of corn at the other guy's back. This would start something like a snowball fight. Only corn is harder than most snow!

A tool used for corn picking was a husking glove. It was just a leather palm with a steel hook set into it and strapped around the hand and wrist. The hook opened the ears for husking and saved our hands and nails. When the wagon was full enough, we'd climb up and drive to the grain bin or corn crib and begin shoveling in the heavy ears.

My "baby sister" Alice was born in July the summer we worked the road at Mobridge. I don't have many stories about the younger members of the family, but I do remember once I was home helping pick corn and had some fun with Alice. This was in about 1923.

I had backed the picking wagon up to the bin and had just gotten started shoveling when a voice said, "What you gonna do wis all dat torn, Henny?" My baby sister smiled up at me, her little face wreathed in blond curls.

"You mean corn," I said, laughing a little.

Alice scowled. "I said 'torn,'" she replied with spirit.

"That's what I said," I teased. "Torn is for the pigs."

Alice stamped a tiny foot. "I didn't say 'torn.' I said 'torn!'" she raged at me.

Perhaps Mother came from the hen house or some such errand at this time and took Alice with her. I do know that I teased Alice about the "torn" for years, and it became a regular joke with us. I hope she has enjoyed it as much as I have.

(One of the last times my dad ate at Alice's house, he asked if she was serving "torn," I don't know if she had planned to, but she opened a can of corn. They were still enjoying the joke. ~ Marlys Denholm)

One time I came home from wherever I was working to find the three little sisters, Ella, Edna and Alice in a very stormy mood. The family had a phonograph, a marvelous machine with a crank and a spring to wind up. There were a few records of the then popular songs and a large "morning glory" horn to carry the sound. Les and Bill, then teenagers, were in their room getting ready to go to a dance. They had taken the phonograph and closed their door. The little girls weren't being let in.

"Well now," I said, "if you sit down and be quiet, you can hear the music. But if you hammer at the door and yell, then you can't hear it." They didn't like the idea much to begin with, but they sat quietly for a while. I guess watching the record go around was half the fun of the music. The family enjoyed the machine, just this time things had gone badly.

Sometime in 1923, our youngest brother George was born. It wasn't long until we knew that Georgie wasn't a healthy baby. The poor little guy just lay still; he didn't seem interested in anything. He never cooed or smiled or learned to sit up. Early in 1924, before he was a year old, our little brother suddenly passed on. Hilda and I were at a friend's dance when someone came to tell us we should go right home.

George, Edward and Christoff are in unmarked graves in the Lemmon cemetery. There was never money for markers.

It was the summer of 1925 that a letter came saying that Mother's sister was ill. Our Aunt Anna was so weak she could hardly get out of bed, Marie wrote, but the doctor could find no cause. "I should go help take care of her," Mother said. "It says they're taking turns."

"The train is running. We can afford the few dollars for a trip," Dad told her. Mother took Ella with her this time. She would be company for Elsie. Good-hearted and efficient Hilda became our chief cook and housekeeper as well as caregiver for Alice, Edna and Don.

Harvest time came with the extra men to cook for, and Hilda's friend, Clara Hoefling, came to help. One day Hilda wanted to serve pie. She wanted it to be good, for one Fred Baumeister was on the threshing crew. We had no way of keeping meat in hot weather and we hadn't butchered, so the girls were short on lard. They went ahead and made pie – with too little lard for crusts.

That pie crust was like cardboard! The girls blushed and giggled as Fred sawed away at his pie. We all had the same trouble, but that didn't matter. After some teasing the story came out. The pie didn't dim Fred's feelings for my sister; she became Mrs. Baumeister the next year. Clara became Mrs. Louie Miller a bit later.

Our aunt became weaker and more poorly, and Mother knew she must be getting home so Ella could go to school. There were things to do to get ready for winter, so Mother told her sister goodbye and took the train home.

Sometime after Aunt Anna's death, Dad read an article about a man who was completely helpless, yet the doctors could find no cause. Someone suggested he have his teeth pulled. The man agreed; he had nothing to lose. The teeth were pulled although they appeared in good condition. And the man recovered to live several years. Our parents were sure then that the good teeth had taken the man's and Aunt Anna's strength. Few doctors or dentists would like this theory.

Uncle Charlie Lang, who had lived in North Dakota for many years, passed away in spring of 1929. There had been a lot of rain, and we pulled Louie's car with horses all the way out to Highway 73 where Louie, Clara, and our folks headed north to Highway 12 to go to the services in Sanborn, North Dakota.

Our mother almost always knew where we were and what we were about, as well as who we were seeing. She was plenty disgusted when a neighbor's girl surprised her parents by getting married and then telling them about it. "No kid of mine ever better do that!" Mother fussed. "Any kid of mine gets married and not tells me first, – I'll kick 'em out! Well, mine wouldn't do that."

Hilda did just that, and Mother was very upset with her and Fred. Hilda had been working in Lemmon and had brought her new things home and sneaked them in through her bedroom window. Then she and Fred went to Bison to be married at the courthouse as was the custom. Hilda came home and announced to her parents, "Well, he's mine now!"

That was a terrible blow to Mother's pride! Dad called Hilda aside and told her, "Let Mama have her say now and you'll see, in a day or so she'll be happy about the whole thing." So Mother had her "say," and just as Dad predicted, she forgave the young folks. Our parents were always good about backing us up and not meddling in our lives.

Alice and Edna had some trouble with Fred. The little girls had to bring coal from a shed to the house each day. They used a small sled to haul the heavy pails. One winter when the Baumeisters stayed with the folks for a while, Fred would sneak up and step on the runners and hold the sled down while the little sisters were hauling coal. Edna might stand smiling shyly or just leave, but Alice continued to pull at the sled all the while yelling at Fred. She had plenty of older "teachers" and could give him some awful tongue lashings! Fred helped the little girls after teasing them, and I doubt if they really minded so much.

Before the little girls started to school, Fred and Hilda moved to a farm north of the folks' farm. Sometimes Alice and Edna went to spend a few days with the Baumeisters. One time the little sisters climbed up in the hayloft and perched on a narrow shelf along the track, high up near the peak of the roof. When Fred and Hilda came to the barn to milk they could hear whispering and giggling. Finally Alice could stand it no longer, "Can't you see us? Look up! Look up!"

Hilda looked. "Oh, no! What'll I tell Ma!"

"How do you figure to get down?" Fred boomed.

"Like this," Alice returned, and she jumped down between braces and two-by-sixes only a couple feet apart. It's a near miracle that she missed all the cross-members and bounced into the hay.

Edna was willing to let Fred get a ladder and help her down. After that Fred might invite the little girls to go home with them, "If you promise not to climb anything," he'd chuckle.

-21-
LAST YEARS ON THE FARM

In every family group there are some things that become regular remarks. I would like to share some of ours.

If someone absent-mindedly took more bread when he still had some, "Somebody hungry coming."

If we had a sore tongue, Mother said, "You must have told a lie."

If you dropped a piece of tableware, "Company coming."

You dropped the dishcloth, "Somebody sloppy coming."

The dog howled, "Someone we know died."

If your ears rang, "Somebody talking about you."

If someone talked silly or smarty, Mother would say not to be "dumb-smart" and that meant no more foolishness.

Our mother simply couldn't understand the idea of vitamins. When the young mothers began giving the little tots few fried foods and more vegetables, Mother shook her head, "My, my, what's to eat is to eat."

An old friend often said of a small glitch or problem, "If that's the worst thing, it's a good day."

As with anything new, a farm truck was considered a foolish luxury by those who did not have one. One of the amusing tales of the late 1920s or early 1930s concerned a bull and a truck. The people involved were going to haul a bull to town for sale. The old way would have been to herd him and other cattle along with a saddle horse or to tie him to a wagon and lead him with a team. To haul an animal seemed utter foolishness.

Apparently the bull thought so, too, and he refused to enter the truck. So the farmer called his sons to get the big team and to bring up the wagon and a hayrack. The men spread the hay ropes or slings used to carry hay into the mow outside the lower barn door. These ropes ran through a system of pulleys and a sturdy team pulled at the far end to raise the hay or other load.

The truck, wagon and rack were positioned to form a small pen. "Now when he comes out of the barn, he'll have to stand over the ropes. You pull him up and I'll back the truck under him. You let him down into the truck." That sounded easy enough. The big son would drive the pulling team, the father would back the truck and the younger son would shoo the beast out of the barn.

All was ready. The bull warily stepped outside and the door was quickly slammed behind him. Trapped in the small enclosure, he was even more surprised to be hauled, much against his will, into the air by the horses at the far end of the pulley rope.

Bedlam broke loose! The bull roared and struggled. The dog set up a great barking. The farmer revved up the truck to back it under the protesting bull. All this was too much for the horses. They bolted ahead, jerking the bull up and into the haymow door. The second son grabbed the trip rope used for dumping the hay load. He pulled, hoping to stop the bull's ride before he went through the far wall of the barn. The trip worked fine and dropped the animal neatly into the barn loft. That was too much! The farmer got his gun and shot the bull, and the story goes, "They butchered him right there."

I hope the Johnson family won't object if I tell a story about Henry Johnson. He was on the threshing crews for many years. Mr. Johnson was a little fellow about our dad's age, and he was a natural clown. Once in about 1931 or 1932, he was having dinner at the farm along with the large number of men who followed the threshing rig. This time Louie's wife, Clara, was helping Mother, and she had their children, Arlene and Duane with her.

Mr. Johnson loved children, and soon he was showing them little tricks. He did things like suddenly "finding" a penny in a boy's ear or folding a finger and saying, "Oh, it fell off." Kids of all ages loved him and remembered him.

There was no running water at the farm so there was a big stone crock with fresh water hauled from the well. On the other side of the wash stand sat the "slop" or waste water to be carried outside.

"Which pail do I drink from?" Mr. Johnson asked the children. They pointed to the crock. "Why not this?" he indicated the other pail. The little folks turned up their noses and looked horrified. Conversation stopped and everyone watched Mr. Johnson and Louie's children.

"You don't drink this?" The little man took the dipper and pretended he would drink from the wrong pail. Men chuckled and the ladies stood watching and smiling while he let the children convince him to drink the good water.

By 1939, we older boys and Hilda had left home, and the dry thirties had hit. Costs rose and profits sank until Dad sold out to the government and moved the family into Lemmon. There is a sad little story in connection with the folks selling the farm.

When the grasshoppers came, they ate everything in sight. The green plants went first, then clothes on the line, paper, leather, even fence posts were chewed. The ugly insects just appeared one morning, and by noon the countryside was laid waste.

Dad had a green climbing vine along the porch east of the farm house. He was very proud of that vine and carefully watered it to keep it growing. When the hoppers came, Dad took a rolled-up newspaper and went out to protect his vine. "The critters can have the rest, but they ain't gettin' my 'wine'!" he said.

Louie and Clara lived on the farm just north of the school, and they had stopped and talked to Dad on the porch when they went into Lemmon. A few hours later when they returned, the beautiful vine was gone. Our dad sat with his head in his hands, a beaten man.

This may well have been the turning point in the decision to sell and retire. The land is now part of the West River National Grasslands and there is not even a windmill tower to mark where the homestead once was.

Bill Miller family members in 1936 or 1937. Clara, Ella, Hilda, Edna, Lester, Fred, Henry, Mother Carrie, Louie, Evelyn, Alice, Dad Bill, and Don. Probably taken by brother Billy. Children would be Arlene, Duane, Loren, Shirley and Bobby Miller, and Verne and Gene Baumeister.

Bill and Carrie Miller's 50th Anniversary in 1948. Don, Ella, Henry, Edna, Alice, Louie, Hilda, Billy, and Lester. Bill and Carrie are seated.

Carrie and William Miller at a picnic in about 1948.

West part of DeWitte Township
and part of east Siem Township

6

5

State Highway 73 North

7

8

18

17

Summer-
ville

19

20

Dam

Park
area,
Game
Reserve

Shade-
hill

and
Reservoir

Grand

River

Hugh Glass Monument-

Two Miles West

From A Soddy

East Part of DeWitte Township, 1970's

-Part B-
STORIES FROM HENRY'S BROTHERS AND SISTERS

Compiled by Marlys Miller Denholm

Hilda Miller Baumeister
Louie C. Miller
William (Bill) F. Miller
Alice Miller Holdal

-1B-
HILDA MILLER BAUMEISTER

Aunt Hilda Miller Baumeister remembers: Uncle Charlie and Mother and we children went into Lemmon in perhaps the spring of 1909. We took along an old maid homesteader neighbor. I don't remember that she was a special friend, but it was a kindness to do this for a woman alone.

When we got back to her place, the woman thanked us and took her things into her shanty. Before we got turned around in her yard, she came out yelling that there was someone in her bed.

Mother and Uncle Charlie went into the house with her. The next minute our uncle came out carrying a big round fence post! The woman said someone must have put into her bed to frighten her. But our uncle and parents wondered if she hadn't put it there herself to get our uncle to come into her house.

* * * * *

We had to carry our drinking water to school when we were small. We each had a fruit jar to carry and keep for ourselves. One of our teachers didn't bother to bring water, but helped himself to our jars of water. This was bad enough, but he was a tobacco chewer! More often than not, he let some chewings seep into our water jars.

How sick we got if we didn't watch for this! Once the water was spoiled, we didn't dare drink for the rest of the day unless a friend or our brothers offered us some of their water.

This man kept a can for a spittoon somewhere away from his desk, then he would spit into it from behind the desk. I don't remember him ever missing.

* * * * *

The grassy, windy country was bad for prairie fires, especially in the years before much land was plowed. Once there was a big fire somewhere north of the farm and the men took teams and plows and went to help stop it. After that people began plowing a few furrows around the pastures and homes for fire guards.

One day we were coming from the school over west and saw smoke ahead. "Grass fire!" Chris yelled. We rounded a little knoll and could see a small fire moving along the creek. Little brother, Louie, stood watching it. He had come to meet us like he often did, and while he waited, he set a tuft of grass afire. We soaked our jackets in the creek and put that fire out. It must have been quite a small fire or we couldn't have stopped it alone.

Another time after Christoff was gone, we took stock to the creek to water. The little boys had some matches they had picked out of Dad's ash tray, and they got a fire started along the creek. We carried water up in a pail we used to water calves and drowned the fire. It was a windy day, and we were mighty tired and scared before we got that fire out!

 * * * * *

One day at breakfast, Dad poured thin chokecherry syrup over his pancakes and said to Mother, "You pick me some more of these sour little devils, and I'll make some 'vine.'"

Mother took a dim view of drinking. "Oh, what for you want 'vine?'" she asked.

But we kids, or some of us, helped Mother pick, carry home, wash and cook the chokecherries. Then Mother strained the juice into large crocks.

Dad took over and added the sugar and yeast as he had read in some paper or heard in town. The crocks were set into the cellar to "work" at making wine.

A few days later, Mother said, "You better look at what your 'vine' is doing. I don't know about that stuff."

"What's it doing?" Dad asked.

"Foaming up all over the place," Mother told him.

Dad went down to the cellar and looked at his wine project. He came up shaking his head and searched in his papers for information on the subject. The wine foamed more and smelled worse. In a few days Dad decided that it was spoiled and he carried it all upstairs and dumped the wine makings out. I guess he just wasn't a wine maker.

* * * * *

When I was about thirteen and Hank was sixteen, the folks took the little kids to the fair. We were to take care of the place and do the evening chores. Then we could go into town for the evening.

That's not how it turned out. Hank took Pa's old corncob pipe and had to try smoking that. He got sicker than a dog! I was so angry with him because he was too sick to help and I milked all the cows myself. Then we had to stay home besides. We never told the folks for years. Kids didn't tell on each other then. We didn't anyway.

* * * * *

When our mother was busy with the new baby in the spring of 1916, it fell to me to cut Les, Eddy and Billy's hair. They were about three, four and six, and I was about thirteen years old. I'd had little or no practice. Mother said they must have a haircut before the school picnic.

It took quite a while and the boys were restless. Bill got tired and he wiggled and wouldn't sit still, and I was getting tired of him and the job. After I scolded him and our mother talked to him, and he still couldn't hold still, I said, "I'll fix you!" And I chopped out a chunk of hair right down to the scalp in the middle of his head! Our parents were plenty disgusted with both of us and it did look awful until the hair grew in. I did learn to cut hair, and Bill did learn to sit still.

* * * * *

When we were young, there were no jeans for girls. If we had to help in the field or do chores in cold weather, we wore our brother's overalls and our mother wore Pa's. Our parents called them "overhauls." No girl or woman let anyone see her wearing "pants" though, except the family. Once when I was about ten years old, a neighbor came to talk to Pa when I was helping shock grain. I was wearing Hank's or Chris' overalls and had to hide behind a wagon until the man left.

By the time I was in the teens, girls would be seen wearing pants for working or riding, but not to town or to school. Mother was old-fashioned and didn't wear "overhauls" except in severe weather.

Hank and I often went to the barn dances and house parties by ourselves when we were teenagers. Some girls rode horseback because it was faster, and I liked to ride so we did that some of the time. When you rode horseback to a party, you wore a blouse and your brother's jeans. A skirt and petticoats and maybe a hair ribbon went into a cloth bag that had drawstrings on it. This was called a "war bag" and we carried it on the saddle.

Once we rode with some friends to a house party, and we girls went behind a small building to change into our skirts. We could have changed in the house, but we didn't. Our brothers would keep watch while we changed. Boys had more respect then; no one would be funny or try to peek. It was dark anyway.

After we'd been dancing a while, my friend stopped me when she and her partner danced by. Her face was red and she was giggling. "Look, I got my skirt on inside out," she whispered. We excused ourselves and went out to change the skirt. We laughed the rest of the night, and for a long time afterwards all the girls were extra careful to get the seams on the inside when they dressed in the dark.

* * * * *

Henry was the best brother a girl could have. He always looked after me at dances and such. Even when we were older and some guy would ask to see me home, I asked my brother. Mostly he said okay, but sometimes he'd say, "Better come with me." I didn't argue; he knew those fellows.

One winter I had measles and mumps and colds so I was ill most of the winter. Different times I knew there were parties or dances, and I'd tell Hank to go. He's say no, he had something he wanted to read, or somebody small needed help with their homework. But I knew he stayed home because I felt bad that I couldn't go. He was always good to us younger ones and looked after our welfare.

One time when we were about grown, Hank and Louie played a mean trick on me. They came from chores and said, "Let's go over to the April Fool dance at Siem." I loved to dance, so I said I'd like that, and we all went to get ready.

I waited and waited for my brothers, and finally I knocked on their door. "Come in," they both said. I opened the door to see Hank and Louie in bed! There I was, dressed up for a dance and my brothers had gone to bed. Oh, I was angry, and they both laughed at their big joke!

* * * * *

I wanted desperately to go on to high school. I loved school and loved to read. But Dad asked, "Can they teach you how to patch "overhauls" there? Of course not!" And I didn't go. Oh the tears I shed as I saw the Hoefling girls and other friends going on to school!

Alice and Edna began school together about the time I was married. Then they came to stay in town with my family to go to high school when the time came. Alice got rheumatic fever and couldn't go on. How the poor girl suffered with that! She was so sore that she cried just from the weight of the blankets.

Edna is the only one of the family to have finished high school. What a fight she had to be allowed to stay in school!

* * * * *

I remember once when our mother was in bed with a new baby, that Hank and Dad helped with the dishes. Our dad grumbled that we must not have done dishes for a week. He thought what he saw on the table was all there were!

-2B-
LOUIE C. MILLER

Uncle Louie C. Miller remembers: I was just a little guy when the family came to South Dakota, so the early homestead stories I know have been told to me. There are a few things so far missed that I think worth mentioning. Some are interesting and some just funny.

You will notice on the map that some quarters of land appear to have two families on them. This is often the case of one party leaving and another taking over. The Erickson-Backman place on 23 was homesteaded by Erickson and later taken over by a brother-in-law, Backman. On 24, the northeast quarter was homesteaded by a Miss Adams and later bought by Wagners. This is now my home place. The Hamlins came in about 1909 to the southwest quarter of section 11, and the Frerkings took over that land in about 1916.

There is a bit of a story about section 24. This was the homesteads of two couples, grandparents of our boyhood friend, Dave Hamlin, and of two maiden aunts. The homesteads were located close together so the ladies had fire protection and transportation. I believe they shared a common well.

The Goerderts lived where the Hamms live now, and Mr. Goerdert was the community violinist. The name was pronounced "Gator." You will notice that a Backman place is located right on the section line. This man is said to have worked the mines at Lead, then homesteaded and returned to Sweden for his bride. Sometime later when the area was more properly surveyed, they learned that the home was built right on the section line.

The Snodgrass on section one was a brother I think, of the Miss Snodgrass who taught at our sod school. She may have stayed there, but her parents lived farther north. The Hamlin and Norton children who went to school with us were cousins.

Hamlins lived over east on 13, so they had a long way to go to the sod school. The two Wheaton places belonged to a couple and their grown son.

The story is told, and I know where the land lies, of a man who homesteaded, instead of a square quarter section, a series of small plots totaling 160 acres along the Grand River. He had hopes of having lush pasture and fields, but got instead the annual flooding and all its problems.

Homestead jokes and stories include a fellow who, when asked by the agent if he had plowed the required 10 acres, said he had plowed "around ten acres." The agent found that the homesteader had picked a chunk of about 10 acres and had plowed around it – once. A well was a requirement, and it is said that some set a barrel into the ground and hauled water from a creek to fill it. This they passed off to the inspector as a well!

Some who had no intention of living on the homestead land built shanties on skids and pulled them to the homestead for inspection and then took them somewhere else. It is even said that such a "home" could be rented for this purpose.

Much is said of the midwife in some pioneer stories. It seems that it wasn't all that big a deal. I think the father most often delivered the baby, then he went to get the neighbor woman who washed the infant and helped the mother clean up. She may have stayed the day to be sure things were going all right. Most times one or another neighbor woman would come and bring a little gift and something cooked or baked over the next few days. She might sweep up and do whatever dishes there were if there wasn't an older child to do that.

I remember once when I wasn't very big our dad sent us all to do the chores and he stayed in the house. After a while he came and told us that there was a new baby in our family. Then he went and got a neighbor lady.

Even in later years, people only called the doctor if things were going badly. The father or big brother rode horseback into town as that was quickest. Then he'd come with the doctor to show him the way.

Dr. Totten had one of the first cars in the Lemmon area. It is told that a young father went to get him late one day and rode in the open car over rough roads at near break-neck speeds back to the farm. Somewhere along the way the doctor decided he needed his headlights on, but he couldn't find the switch. "The hell with that!" he exclaimed, and stepped on the gas all the more.

* * * * *

Horses were important to the settlers. They were our power and our transportation, and if properly treated and cared for, our friends. Dad brought four horses from Minnesota, and our pet riding pony came with them. There is a sad story about that pony. After we had been in Perkins County for a while we boys were out with our dad when he was building fence one spring. The older boys were running errands for our dad while he worked. Fencing is not an altogether safe operation, so I would have been in the wagon out of the way.

The pet pony was running loose and grazing along where we were. Suddenly we heard pounding hooves, loud shouts and gun shots! The team reared and would have run away, but Dad was right there to hold them. "Get that kid outta the wagon!" he yelled to my brothers.

I was jerked out of the wagon by Christoff and Hank who hustled me to what they hoped was a safe spot. Chris ran to help hold the horses and Hank tried to comfort me. The cowboys rode past, shooting and whooping and headed in a south-westerly direction. Our pony ran west over the hills and was never seen again by any of us.

* * * * *

The spring and summer of 1911 were terribly dry. Dad took four horses and the hay mower and rake to North Dakota to cut hay for the winter. Mother and we boys were left with the milking chores, herding cattle and a few hogs and a pitiful garden to look after. I say "we" because by then I was old enough that I was expected to be of some help.

About noon on August 18 (for some reason that date has stuck in my mind), the sky got dark and Mother began her rounds. Our mother had a great fear of storms, especially if she and we children were alone. "Finish your food now," she coaxed as she went from one window to the next checking the sky on every side. I don't think Mother ate a thing, maybe a slice of bread, as she went around again studying the sky for signs of a tornado. When she came from the bedroom Mother had a couple quilts over her arm.

"Are we going to the cellar, Ma?" Christoff asked.

"Sure, what'd you think?" Hank teased.

"None of that," Mother said sharply. "Now Hilda get the bread into a towel. You boys take that and the quilts down in case we have to go." Mother went to look after baby Eddy and the older children hurried to do as she had instructed. I helped Billy down from his chair and washed both our faces. Hilda was clearing the table.

The boys were back. "The wind's really whipping, Ma," Chris said.

"And it's cold like it could hail," Hank told us.

Mother put a blanket around the baby and picked up a bundle of diapers. "Hank, bring Billy. Christoff, you see everything's tight here." Mother had opened the windows to help equalize air pressure and maybe save the house in case of a tornado, but doors would be closed so they wouldn't be torn from their hinges by strong winds.

We went out into a cold wind and Christoff closed the doors. He and I ran to open the door to the storm cellar. This was perhaps ten feet from the house. I padded barefoot down the cool stone steps and turned to watch the family come down – Mother and the baby, Hank and little Billy, Hilda with the kerosene lantern. I heard Chris slam the upper door and fasten it. He was coming down the steps when Hank struck a match on the seat of his pants and lit the lantern. Chris closed the lower door and we all looked around.

Mother sat on a chair with the baby on her lap. "Make yourselves comfortable," she sighed. "It may be a long afternoon." Our big brothers had spread the quilts on the two-foot-wide shelves that ran around three sides of the cellar. They helped us smaller ones and Hilda jump up and sat beside us.

Chris turned to Mother, "Is there cream in that?" He poked his toe at the crock churn with the long stick stomper. "I may as well churn a little for you."

"That would be fine," Mother was pleased. I was more than pleased! It was I who all too often had to churn with that old stomper. I suppose that everyone was at some time the right age and size for churning, but how I hated the job! Once I got a notion that if I slopped around and made a real mess maybe Mother would decide that I was just too little and couldn't churn. That's not how it worked out.

We hadn't been in the cellar very long when we heard thunder. We couldn't hear much rain, hail or wind from below the ground. Little Billy and the baby went to sleep, and Mother told stories about when she was a girl in Iowa and Illinois. After while Mother told Christoff to open the lower door. With that open, we could hear the pounding of rain and hail on the little building above.

Chris shut the door, and we all sat down. Mother told Hank to blow out the lantern to save air. We didn't call it oxygen, just "air." The boys practiced their spelling and numbers a while in the dark. It seemed like a long time until the boys opened the door again. It was still raining.

Chris lit the lantern, and Mother cut bread for us. One of the boys probably buttered it with his pocket knife. And we had milk to drink. Mother kept lunch things and cups in the cellar. The lunching helped pass time and we felt better. Edward woke up and Mother nursed him, then he sat on her lap and we played with him a bit.

"Take a look once more," Mother nodded toward the door. The big boys, eleven and twelve years old, opened the door. All was quiet above! My brothers ran up the steps and listened again at the upper door. Hilda and I crowded into the lower doorway, and Mother stepped over to where she could see and hear Hank and Chris.

"Ma, come and look! Water everywhere!" "Oh man, the frogs and toads!" "The house is still here," the boys called down. We raced up the steps to see. Mother wrapped the baby and climbed the steps to look outside. We boys hopped barefoot in the puddles, splashing around until Mother told us to quit that. If she wanted to be wet she'd have gone out in the rain. Hilda fussed and squealed as the frogs hopped out of our way. Maybe Chris helped her and Hank kept Billy from falling into a puddle.

Inside the house we wiped our feet on one of the rag rags in the shed and again in the kitchen. "Be careful. Stay right there," Mother commanded. She handed Hilda the baby, set Billy on a chair, and snatched up her broom from the corner by the stove. I looked around as Mother went about sweeping up broken glass. Several windows were gone, and some newspapers and other light things were blown about and rain wet.

Mother got Hilda's shoes from the bedroom. "Put them on and help me," she said. Mother put the baby on my lap. "Stay there now," she said to both of us. To the older boys, Mother said, "You fellows best be seeing to the stock." It was already chore time.

Several days after the big rain, the long overdue oats and corn were coming up in the August heat. Everything – fields, pastures and creek bottoms, were green and growing! Some garden came up, but seeds had blown away or sprouted and died.

One of the neighbors, I think Mr. Wagner, rode past one day and he stopped to see how we were getting on. This man told us that a tornado had gone past only four miles north of our farm. "Blew the feathers right off some of Hoefling's chickens," he said.

"That fellow west of there lost his water tank. It blew into the hole where a house had been. Funny thing, that water wasn't even spilled. There it was, the tank nearly full, sitting in a hole!" He shook his head. "Sure something! Three quarters of a mile it went."

"You know that pole shed over there built into a hill?" he asked the boys. Yes, they'd herded up there. "Well, there was a claim shanty about a half mile west of there. Now the shanty's in the hole in the hill, all in one piece. And the shed's plum gone." He looked at the house. "You lost some windows. Everything else okay? Can we help any?"

Mother said no, we were getting along fine. She had tacked some boxes over the open windows and the cows were milking better on the new grass. We could trade some butter for glass. "It'll be a slim winter, but we're better off than many." Mother was usually cheerful and optimistic. She said again how fortunate we were and how thankful we should be to have escaped the tornado.

* * * * *

The next summer one of the boys herded cattle and the other helped in the fields. The cowherd used the miserable mule, so the animal was in the corral or the small night pasture. One day the mule had tried to make friends with a little calf or somehow had got an old cow angry with him. The cow got Jack into a fence corner and gave him a good jab in the ribs with a long horn.

We came in the morning to hear poor Jack wheezing and squeaking. He couldn't bray! It wasn't many days until the soreness left and Jack was braying loudly again at the dawn, the morning milkers and anything else that caught his eye. A mule has an awful voice. He seems to pump out all his wind and then have trouble catching his breath.

Jack was all through with cows, and the next time he was put into the pasture, he crawled through the fence into a horse pasture. This belonged, I think, to Myron Delap. This man had some thirty horses of various ages and sizes, and Jack raced toward them expecting a warm welcome no doubt.

The horses took fright at the loud braying and ran. The fool mule followed and brayed, and the whole herd began running around and around along the fence. When the horses came to a corner, Jack caught up a little by cutting across, and things got worse all the time. Before very long, the horses were crowding into the inch-long barbs of the fence. Wires broke, horses got cut up and the herd started cross the prairie.

The neighborhood fathers saw dust or heard the commotion and some men went out and stopped the trouble. Pa and my brothers spent several days fixing the man's fence. We had to pay for some horses that had died or had to be destroyed, too. This was quite a blow to the family economy. Our pa traded the mule off as soon as he could. Luckily there was quite a demand for jacks in those days.

Some fear a mule is mean. They aren't usually, but a mule can kill a stallion half again his size. Most mules are lazy, but they can do a lot of work on poor feed.

* * * * *

From A Soddy

In 1912 when I began school, we were at the sod school a mile west of the homestead. Jim Keller was our teacher. There were mice in a soddy left for a year like that, and sometimes even a snake. Early in the fall one day we had the door open when we became aware of an odor. Our teacher told us to "keep quiet and move slowly over there" toward the far wall. That was away from the large skunk that had come calling. The animal came right into the building and a bunch of frightened children moved right out! The rest of the day we had school out in the sunshine.

One term we had school in a claim shanty a mile south of the homestead where a Mr. Carlson had lived. This shanty became the kitchen of the house years later when I lived there with my family. In the mid-1940s Hank bought the farm, and later I bought it from him. The house stood until 1948.

In 1915, a frame school building was moved in from somewhere north. The man who did the moving had four of the biggest horses I have ever seen. I was nine or ten at the time, and I remember him pitching hay to those horses until I wondered if they'd ever have enough. The mover stayed the night with us, so I got to see the animals at work. I was used to big horses, but I especially remember these. I think their heads were a yard long.

Christoff never went to this school, and Hank probably took only his seventh grade in the new school. The rest of the family finished the eight grades here. We had a lot of good times at school, but we knew why we were there, too. Jim Keller was our teacher several years. Another was Mrs. Emberson who still lives in Lemmon.

When I think of school I always have to think of Johnny Dunn. Every school has a clown and he was a favorite. When Mr. Keller came to teach he asked us all our names.

Then to be sure he had them right in his mind, he asked different ones again. "You are Mr. Dunn?" he asked of Johnny.

Johnny tipped his chair back and said, "Yes, and I don't think I'll ever get done."

We laughed. Mr. Keller was a good sport and let us have some fun.

Once Johnny caught a high ball and remarked, "Wow! That hurts a man's hands!"

Hank said, "How would you know? You are a boy." We teased Johnny about that, but he could take our kidding. He was the only one in school who knew how to catch a rattlesnake. He'd cut out its fangs with his pocket knife and then play with the snake.

One time we saw a skunk go under the school building, so we older guys plugged up his entrance with dirt, hay and grass. We went inside and didn't say a word about our prank. After while our walking about combined with not being able to escape was too much for the skunk. The terrible odor seeped up through the floor, and we looked at one another, wondering what our teacher would do or say. It wasn't long until we were told that school was over for the day.

In 1918 almost everyone failed in school. This was the year of the bad flu epidemic. I was in the eighth grade that year and passed only part of my subjects. After Thanksgiving the next fall I came back to finish the credits I had missed so I could get my diploma in the spring.

* * * * *

Most young folks don't know what "riding fence" means, but it was a job a ten-year-old boy could do and enjoy. You take a pocket full of staples and a hammer and ride horseback along the pasture fences. If you see a loose wire, you staple it back on the post. Posts were all wood cut from the trees along the creek or near the river. I'd bang each post with my hammer as I passed. This made an interesting "singing" in the wires.

I checked on water supplies and looked for hurt or sick animals. If there was a problem, a boy had better be able to tell his pa about it and where to find it.

On several occasions I'd see a rattlesnake. I climbed off my horse and killed the snakes with the hammer when I was older. If one can keep the snake scared and moving away it's pretty easy to kill. You have to catch him before he coils. I have killed them with a wrench since I was grown. It's a strange thing how they always seem to try to turn and fight Hank or Pa, but most snakes would run from me.

This is not to say a rattlesnake isn't dangerous. He is! Some folks think that western South Dakota is so infested with snakes that one hardly dares get out of the car. This is not the case. There are more snakes some places than in others. When you live near a danger you learn to automatically watch for it. On a cool day the snakes like to be on the sunny side of logs, stones and porches of a house sometimes. When it's hot, look for the snake in the shade.

I've pitched a snake onto a load of hay and ridden home in the hay wagon with him. This was purely an accident and when the rattler was found, I shook. It's a wonder he didn't fall on my head when I pitched him up!

There are often more rattlesnakes on a high stony hill than on lower ground. The hill near the school was a bad place for snakes; we even had one in the house once.

We had one on the south porch at the Wagner place once. Considering how many snakes have been seen and killed in the area, it's a wonder more people haven't been bitten.

Rattlesnakes "den up" or hibernate in a high hill for the winter and anyone coming upon the den site when the snakes are coming out in the spring had best be well prepared. Snake hunts are sometimes held at this time and the snakes are "milked" for venom to make the anti-venom vaccine and then killed.

Larger animals like the cattle and horses are rarely affected by one snake bite. In grazing, the animal may get too near or surprise the snake and so be bitten. We have had a horse going around with his face all swelled up, and then be fine again in a few days. But anyone unknowingly riding onto the snake den was lucky to save his horse.

Rattlesnakes live on rats, mice, cottontail rabbits and gophers, so they have a place in nature. We have to be careful not to leave piles of junk and such that will attract rodents to a farm, since these then attract the snakes.

* * * * *

After Christmas, beginning in about 1916, we cut ice on the Grand River. A team and sled were driven onto the river. Then men took iron bars and chipped out a hole in the ice. An ice saw was used to cut a block of ice about two-feet square and as deep as the ice had frozen at the time. A wooden trough or chute ran from the hole in the ice up to the rear of the sled. As each ice block was cut loose, tongs were clamped onto it and several men pulled the block up the chute and into the sled.

When the sled was loaded it was pulled home where we unloaded the ice into what was known as the ice house. An old soddy with its thick walls made a good ice house. Rocks or timbers were laid on the floor first, and the ice stacked on top. When the ice did melt a little the water dripped away. Ice didn't melt so fast when it didn't stand in water.

The first blocks of ice slid in the door and were arranged. We couldn't lift the ice, so the next load was pulled chunk by chunk up the chute and dropped in through a hole in the roof. Ice was stacked only to two or three feet from the walls of the building.

This space was filled with straw or old hay and trampled down tight to make insulation. The huge blocks of ice inside had been fit tightly together to keep air from circulating around them. When the building was full, or we had as much ice as we expected to need, the ice was well covered with straw and the trap door replaced on the roof.

The ice was used a chunk at a time in summer in Mother's ice box. The ice box was an old fashioned refrigerator set in the pantry or cellar. There were shelves for food and a shelf or box for the ice. A pan lead the drips from the melting ice into a pail below.

It was always good for a little excitement when everybody forgot to empty the pail or thought someone else was going to do it. As soon as we could afford an ice cream freezer we chopped ice to use in the freezing of our own ice cream.

*****

As Hank said, we did quite a lot of herding. When we were older boys we learned roping. We practiced on the cattle we herded, and we had some good roping horses. One horse that I remember was not a roping horse. He refused to lean back on the rope and hold the animal we had lassoed. So for fun, one of us would rope a big old cow or steer from this horse. Then the roper would jump off and run away a safe distance. We'd sit together on the second horse to see the "show."

From a little way off we'd watch the cow and horse fight and struggle against each other and the rope. Soon both animals were down and tangled. The horse might get up to leave only to find that the cow was still dragging at the saddle horn. The horse would begin bucking and kicking at the rope. We laughed and cheered for one and then the other as both went down again. Now the cow was up and running off to join the herd. She'd hit the end of the rope, almost jerking the horse off his feet. Making a fast turn, Mrs. Cow would wrap the rope around the horse's legs and they'd both be down fighting and grunting again.

When both animals were tired, we'd turn the cow loose – and watch out she might charge you! The silly horse always seemed to think we were rescuing him as we coiled up the rope to go about the day's work. I suppose this was mean of us, but we had very little fun in those days.

In 1918 when I was about 13, Dad bought a saddle horse for me. It was just what I wanted, and I expect he went out of his way to get him because I wanted this particular animal so much. One bright day Hank and I rode our old breaking horse down to get my new mount. It was perhaps five miles along the Grand River and east. I rode behind the saddle carrying my tack on my shoulder.

There we tied my prize to the snubbing post in the corral and saddled him. The colt was halter broke, that is you could lead him, but he wasn't trained to ride. After some maneuvering and much coaxing, I was aboard. The halter rope was tied to Hank's saddle horn, I took up the reins, and we were on our way.

This is how we trained our riding horses: I rode the bronc and Hank handled the rope and the training horse and did the coaxing. Hank was very good at making a young horse understand what was expected of him. He could get tough too if the animal didn't behave after it knew better. We traded mounts sometimes, but it worked best if Hank took the training horse and I rode the colt.

Riding the training horse is hard work. If the bronc rears, you have to get yourself and get your mount out of the way so he can get down without hurting anyone. The trainer keeps both horses moving forward, not off to the side and teaches the colt or bronc to stand for mounting and dismounting. A good training horse is a great help at this. These broncs were often three or four years old and hadn't been handled. This is much different from working with a pet that's been eating oats from your hand and wearing a halter since he was a month old.

We didn't just get on and ride for miles. We got on and off, walked around petting the horses and talking to them. Then we got on again to get the bronc used to a man's weight and help him learn to stand. We rode a while, then I'd get down again to help the colt get used to a man's voice and smell. We moved slowly toward home and my legs got red and sore from the rough saddle and the jumping and jerking of the bronc as he shoved and pulled at the other horse. We were fighting less and grinning more as the colt became manageable. We were tired when we got home, but we took a turn around the yard to show off for the family before we put the horses in the barn for the night.

We worked my new horse every day from then on and he made good progress. Then one night we had him in the barn and when morning came he was gone. Vanished! The tie was there, and about a foot of rope. Well, maybe it was chewed, but it looked like knife scrapings to me.

Later I got a big black horse. He was just about the best looking horse I've ever seen, all dark, shiny black and well put together. He was partly broke and Hank and I worked and trained him the same as the others. The day after I got this animal, I rode him out to bring in the work horses. They never came up to the yard so fast before or since!

That bronc got away from me and just ran the work stock all the way. I rode along, but I wasn't in control at all. Mother was really angry with Dad for letting me take a half-broke horse out alone. He probably didn't know until I'd gone. We finished training the colt, and I had a good riding horse for many years.

At the peak of Dad's farming operation, in about 1920, we kept some thirty draft or work horses and five or six saddle stock. There were a couple of light fast buggy teams, but most of the horses were of medium and heavy draft type. Some of the big ones had feet as big around as five gallon pails and appetites to match. During the winter we kept in a light team and a heavy team and usually two saddle horses. These took us to town, hauled hay, coal, and barn cleanings. The rest of the horses roamed the hills and stubble fields and took shelter and some feed at a straw stack.

If snow gets deep and covers fences horses will walk over and leave. Many winters that happened and everyone's working stock was running in a big herd by spring. It was quite a job to corral the lot of them and sort out one's own. In the spring we began feeding a little grain to help the horses stay at home. It does wonders that way, and we had to have them so we could handle them. The grain would help them get in shape for the long days of spring work. Some of the mares would be foaling and then needed a little oats. These mothers might "vacation" until many horses were needed at harvest time. Many colts have been halter broke being led along as their mothers pulled the bundle rack.

Spring was also breaking time. We broke and trained three year olds, but if a colt hadn't been needed, he may have got to four or more before we got to him. A bronc was harnessed along with calm older horse. The pair was hitched to the breaking cart, a rattley cart or light wagon that was easy to get on or off if things went badly. And away we went.

A colt made many fast, false starts, kicked at the wagon tongue, jumped sideways, and in general you didn't know just what might happened next. The old breaking horse walked along holding the colt from going too fast or getting away from us, and kept him moving forward. A colt will know his mother all his life, and she often was the helping horse and had a calming effect on the frightened youngster.

When the colt was tired, we would take off his bridle so he could see the noisy contraption coming behind him. He would be tied by the halter to the other horse. It was better for him to get over his fright now than later when we thought he was trustworthy and had him hitched to a valuable piece of machinery. Now we knew we couldn't trust our bronc so we were on guard.

From A Soddy

One spring we were training a young mare who hated the whole procedure. She got away from us when she was in the pasture. After a few days, Mr. Wagner stopped and told us he thought our horse was there. His description fit the animal, and on the morning of the school picnic, Dad gave me orders to ride to Wagner's and bring the mare home. "Drag her if you have to, but don't come back without her."

That wise and ornery mare wouldn't be chased home, so finally I roped her and dragged her. My saddle horse had to pull her almost all the way. Time I got home, everyone else was gone to the picnic. My horse was tired out, so I saddled the bronc and set out for the picnic a couple miles south along the river.

I led my new mount out of the yard, closed the gate and climbed up. That's the last I remembered until I came to with my head shoved between the boards of the gate. I had an awful time getting my head out of that gate! It's a wonder I didn't get hurt. The mare stood aside looking like she'd like to laugh. That made me mad! "After all the trouble you've given me, you owe me a ride!" I told her. I got on again and this time we got along fine and I rode her to the picnic.

Mother was terribly upset and embarrassed to have me show up riding a half-broke work horse. That evening she let us all know how unhappy she was about me riding "that plow horse for everyone to see."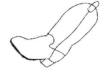

"Aw, let the boy alone," Dad growled as the rest of the family added their teasing and scolding. "Last time you was all away, I saddled the stallion and rode him after the cows."

"You rode him?" Mother stormed, "He's like to kill a person!" That stallion wasn't mean, and we drove him for work, but no one else ever rode him. We trained the bronc and drove her, too. She was too big to ride.

We did some stunt riding, but not with the big horses. We could climb under a running horse's neck, and we all taught our horses to stand so we could run up behind the mount. Hank could hold onto the saddle horn with both hands, hit the ground with his feet, bounce up over the running horse, hit the ground on the other side, then bounce and be mounted. This never worked very good for me. Maybe I got too tall before I got my adult strength. I was the neck and under-the-belly crawler. It helps if you're a skinny kid with a light-built horse. Hilda rode too, and she did some of the less strenuous stunts.

We tried to keep our work horses gentle and trained so we could ride some of them. This came in handy if we needed to go somewhere for a piece of machinery or were leaving a wagon or machine some place. We just rode one of the horses instead of having to walk.

The first summers I worked on the road crew I used four of Dad's horses on the earth scoop called a Fresno. When the noon or supper bell rang, I unhitched all the tugs or traces, let the driving lines drag and climbed onto a horse. While the horses walked toward camp, I hooked up the tugs to the clips on the harness, tied the line, and moved onto the next horse. I hooked tugs and tied lines all the way. Then perched on my last horse, I watched the other fellows hooking tugs and walking up behind their teams. I had my horses fed and watered and was at the cook tent ahead of the rest of the crew.

The first few days the guys would say, "Look at that kid!" and I felt like a celebrity.

On this job, Hank used a great big team of Dad's. He drove them on the water wagon, and they were good. Most horses would jump and jerk if the load didn't come right away, but Hank's team would stand and lean into the collars slow and easy. After a while the big load of water would come up out of the creek, and they'd be on their way to the roadbed. Hank always admired good pulling horses. He bought this team and later trained several more himself.

* * * * *

From A Soddy

In the summer of 1921, Hank and I worked with the road-building crew along what is now U.S. Highway 12. This was in the Wakpala area where the road was built right along the railroad.

A homesteader had a large garden and melon patch in a dip near the tracks and we had been watching the melons ripen all summer. One Sunday, three of us decided to get some watermelon. We walked up the railroad toward the melon patch. There was a boy about fourteen, sitting with a shotgun across his knees. My friends were ready to run. "Let's get out of here!" one said.

"No, now hold on, I got my mouth all set for some melon," I said. "We'll just buy one." We went up to the patch and I gave the boy a quarter for a big melon. We cut it up with our jack knives and walked away down the tracks eating our melon.

The boy went to take his pa the money, and we circled back, and keeping below the level of the tracks, we came back to the melon patch. We took off our shirts and made bags of them by tying sleeves and buttoning the fronts. We filled the shirts with small orange-sized melons and left, keeping out of sight below the tracks.

We came to one of the old fashioned section cars the railroad men used when they checked the tracks. We set the car onto the track, loaded our melons, climbed on and began pumping our way back to camp. The pumping powered the car.

We were going along enjoying ourselves and feeling smart when someone hollered, "Here comes a train!" We stopped and hopped down, lifted the car off the tracks and waited for the train to pass. We waved at the engineer; then when the caboose went past, we threw melons to the train crew standing out on the rear platform. After the train was gone we got back on the section car and rode to camp. We set the car off for the railroad crew to find when they needed it, gave the melons to some Indian women and considered our afternoon lark a success.

When we worked on this road gang, everyone had to take a turn at night hawking. That is herding the working stock at night. This was the only time they could eat. We were expected to take them to good grass to keep up their strength. We worked in pairs, two of us guarding the horses and mules a night, and then it was quite a while until it was our turn again.

One night there was rain, thunder, lightning, and more rain. Two of us younger lads happened to be on herd. We knew there was an Indian Catholic church over away from camp, so we let the stock graze around nearby, and we took turns going inside to get some sleep and try to dry off a little. It was spooky in the big empty building. The lightening would flash and light up the colored windows and the statues.

I napped a while on one of the back pews, then my buddy came in and said the horses were all over among the grave stones. We chased the animals out of the cemetery and then I stayed out and he got some rest. That's the only unusual thing I remember about night hawking.

* * * * *

After harvest late in 1921, our dad came out to work on the road and I went home to take care of things. I got home in October to get acquainted with Alice who had been born in July. Edna was about two; Don maybe five; Ella, seven; Lester would have been about nine; Eddy, ten, and Billy, twelve. Hilda was seventeen or so. This was the summer that Don broke his ankle. There were quite a bunch of children to do things, but the boys were in school. There was still corn to pick and chores to do. So our dad or one of the older boys should be home.

One day I took Lester, Billy, and Eddy out in the farm wagon to pick corn. We had the extra high side boards on for corn, and they always flopped when the wagon was empty. The boys were playing and having a good time when we hit a bump and Eddy hollered. One of those flopping boards had hit him. Then Eddy laughed, so we didn't think he was hurt. Maybe his nose bled a little; it did later.

At supper that night, Eddy said, "That's funny, I bumped my head and my nose bled." After while he told Mother he couldn't see, so she put him to bed with a cold cloth on his head. In a day or so, Eddy was no better so Mother called Dr. Totten. The doctor said meningitis, probably from a concussion, and we better call Dad.

Dad and Hank came on the train for the funeral. No one seems to remember whether they got here before Eddy passed away. It was awfully hard for me, the brother who was in charge, so I don't remember any of the details very well.

Afterwards, someone went back to Wakpala and brought home the horses and wagons for the winter. This may have been the last winter we were all at home. This was Hank, Hilda, me, Billy, Lester, Ella, Donald, Edna, and baby Alice. These are the nine of us who grew up.

* * * * *

Our dad rented or leased quite a lot of land besides what we owned. In 1922 Hank set up farming on the southwest part of section 25 south of the Grand River. We called that the hay farm. One summer I stayed and helped him put up hay.

We had a little pasture there to keep the work stock in. One night there was a lightning storm and in the morning several of our horses were laid out like so many dominoes. It appeared that one was too near the fence when lightening came along the wire. The electricity had passed from one animal to the next and killed four or five of them.

In about the mid-1920s, Dad bought a pair of jennies from Mr. Beal at Chance. The jennies were female mules and were smaller than our saddle horses, but could they travel! We drove them into Lemmon in as little as thirty minutes if we just let them go. The problem came in stopping the little beasts. Fred Baumeister was on the farm helping us one summer, and he and I worked the jennies trying to get them trained so the boys could use them to haul water for the steamer during threshing. No amount of pulling and calling "whoa" would stop the little mules until they were ready to slow down. Fred took a whip and made the jennies run, all the while pulling the lines and calling, "Whoa!" Before long, the jennies were behaving better, but we never could trust them.

That fall, Dad and I were hauling the water tank on a wagon with the jennies. We hauled from a creek, or if we had to, from the well. We topped a little rise, and those pesky mules saw all the teams around the threshing rig. Well, we took off downhill lickety-cut with the full tank of water sloshing and banging along. Dad hauled back on the lines and hollered "Whoa! Easy there," before he switched to strong remarks. I took up the whip and began laying it onto the mules' rumps. Dad lost his temper. "Boy, what's a matter you? Whip 'em when they's already running away with us!"

I kept slapping the jennies and they soon slowed to a trot and then a walk. When we arrived at the thresher, the wicked mules were walking along on their best behavior!

* * * * *

The picking up and selling of buffalo bones and the trapping and selling of muskrat skins were a great help to the family finances of the settlers. We boys trapped for years on every little creek and pond that had a few rat mounds. We got from five to ten cents a pelt. That was good pay for boys then.

After World War II, the game department planted beaver in the area. We objected and said we would shoot the beaver on our land. We were told that this is a federal crime.

In only a few years the muskrats were gone; the trees were cut along the creeks and the lowlands ruined for muskrats. I still believe it was a mistake to bring in the beaver.

-3B-
WILLIAM (BILL) F. MILLER

Uncle Bill F. Miller's humorous contribution: Along in the mid-twenties, our pa bought a car, but he didn't plan to drive it. The boys could do that. We teased and coaxed until he agreed to try driving one day.

We drove around the house with the hand throttle set for a low speed and let Dad take over. It wasn't long until he decided he'd had enough of that. For more fun, we bailed out, leaving him on his own.

"How do you stop this thing?" he demanded. "Whoa! Whoa – you –!"

The family stood on the step to see the show, and instead of stopping the car, our dad just jumped out and let it go. The car didn't do any damage before one of us caught it and parked it. That was Dad's way of letting us know he was no driver of cars.

-4B-
ALICE MILLER HOLDAL

Aunt Alice Miller Holdal remembers: Our older brothers and sister had told Edna and me that no matter how you dropped a cat, it would land on its feet. One day the folks left for town before the older kids came from school and Edna and I were home alone for a little while. We decided to try a daring experiment. We would toss a cat off the windmill tower and see!

I took the cat up the thirty-foot steel tower. Imagine a little kid climbing that tower while carrying a cat! It must have been very tame. Once up the tower, I put the cat on the platform there for the workmen to stand on and climbed up myself.

"Ready? Here she comes!" I threw the cat off the platform. Then I climbed down.

Edna was staring at the cat. It didn't make any difference how she had landed. The cat was stone dead!

We argued about how to get rid of the body, then got a spade and buried the cat behind the barn before the older kids came home. It's a wonder the dog didn't dig it up and come dragging it around.

At milking time we looked in bins and such places that a cat might be shut in. After several days everyone decided that the cat was gone for good. Hank told of finding the body of a white cat in a field one spring, and he suspected that a coyote had taken the cat for a rabbit and killed it, then left it. So the family thought maybe that had happened to our cat, too. We were big girls before we told the story.

* * * * *

We thought we needed a swing. So I climbed up the mill tower with a long lasso rope and tied it to the tail of the windmill. Edna stood below and pulled the rope out to the weight, a cement ball like the old fashioned windmills had. We ran and jumped, swinging on the rope with the little-kid knot I'd tied. We were careful to take little swings and jumps if anyone was around. But when we thought we were alone, we took high jumps and long swings. It's a wonder that knot didn't come undone and drop us!

* * * * *

After our older brothers were away from home, Bill and Lester were the drivers for the family. Dad coached them. I remember one Sunday we were late for church, and Bill was driving. We came tearing up to the old church building on south Main Street in Lemmon. There was no sidewalk and everyone drove up close.

My brother almost didn't get the car stopped before hitting the building. Our dad began to cuss and asked the poor boy if he couldn't drive and if he couldn't he might let someone else try. Doors and windows were open and everyone heard!

When you are late, there is no place to sit except up front. We girls walked in with red faces and hanging heads – all the way up front!

Marlys Miller Denholm

The Venturers
By Evelyn Wampler Miller

On the broad Dakota prairies, around eighteen-seventy-five,
The canvas-covered wagons slowly moved as if alive.
Drawn by patient, plodding oxen, some by horses, two or four.
At times, several came together; at times trains of many more.

Each man found his homestead quarter
 in some way unknown to me.
To a weary, hopeful family, here was home without a tree.
They plowed a furrow, lifted pieces,
 piled them on the chosen site.
Built them up to form their shelter. Worked and planned
 from dawn 'til night.
Built a shelter for their livestock, except for chimney,
 much the same.
Chose a likely spot for water, dug, rejoiced if water came!

Heat of summer, cold of winter, hunger, thirst, but harder still,
Seeing loved ones lie in sickness far from any doctor's skill.
Burying the newborn who didn't utter his first cry.
Burying often without clergy, for it is part of life to die.

This, the life that brings together neighbors, caring each for all.
Wife and husband sharing, sparing, living close.
But closer still is the spirit. No dissension, pettiness, or selfish pride.
Children growing, helping, learning, each one proving true when tried.

How much we owe these early settlers!
 What examples they for us.
If only we knew such contentment and in God had such a trust!

Henry Miller

Henry Miller,
early 1920s.

Henry Miller and
a friend, early 1930s.

Henry Miller and friends in
Yellowstone Park, 1934 or 1935.

Henry and Evelyn Miller
and baby, Marlys, 1938.

Henry Miller's brother, Bill, at the opening to his dugout home in Oak Gulch Township, Day County, about 1939.

Henry Miller's neice, Arlene Miller, left, and his sisters, Ella, Alice, and Edna Miller, about 1939.

Homemade trailer home of Henry and Evelyn Miller, 1939.

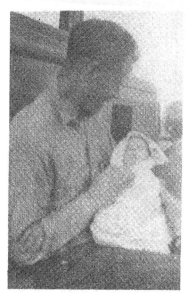

The Family of Henry and Evelyn Miller

**Darrell Edward Miller
born 1939**

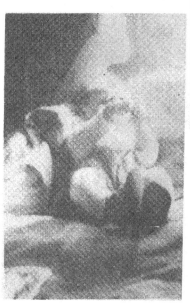

**Left:
David William Miller
born 1940**

**Above: Nyla June Miller
born 1942
with Marlys Ruth Miller
born 1937**

Top: Henry and Evelyn Miller's children, taken about 1943.

Left: Marlys, Darrell, David, and Nyla Miller, taken at school in 1949.

Below: Going to church with Mother in 1952.

**Henry Miller could still stand on his head
in 1957!**

Miller School Building, taken in about 1958.

Graduates

Marlys Miller, 1955

Darrell Miller, 1957

David Miller, 1959

Nyla Miller, 1960

Five and Twenty Years
By Marlys Miller Denholm

Time was – six and twenty years ago -
There was a community show
At a schoolhouse rural.
A gay young farmer met the teacher girl.
That was six and twenty years ago.

Romance bloomed in spring that year.
Neighbors said, "It's for real, I hear."
She said, "Yes." She'd marry her beau
June first – five and twenty years ago.
Happy friends gave many a cheer.

So they wed quite soon
On a sunny first of June.
At a parsonage, brown
In McIntosh town,
Out where the cacti bloom.

Time passed on and new joy was lent.
There came a wee one – blest event!
Oh, happy times and hard times came;
But life and love go on the same.
Said Dad, "These joys are heaven sent."

Marlys Miller Denholm

There came a brother –
And then another.
Fourth, a little sister, sweet.
Said Mom, "Our joy is now complete,
But, oh, I am a busy mother!"

Children grew tall,
Thought they knew it all.
Parents were vexed,
Asked, "Are your manners hexed?"
Oh, it was quite a ball.

Next came grandchildren, dear;
They'll drive you wild, we fear,
With, "Can I have?"
And, "I would like …"
Yet bringing lots of cheer.

Just five and twenty years ago
Could you have known it would be so?
You'd not believed it, anyhow;
But it's all here and real and now.
Life is grand, it goes to show.

Written by Marlys Miller Denholm
in honor of her parents, Henry and Evelyn Miller.
Read by Nyla Miller on the occasion of their
25th wedding anniversary.

Henry and Evelyn's 25th wedding anniversary
was celebrated in 1961 in Bristol. Pictured are
David Miller, Marlys Denholm, Evelyn and Henry,
Nyla Miller, and Darrell Miller.

Taken during the 25th wedding anniversary celebration in
honor of Henry and Evelyn Miller in 1961. Pictured are,
front row from left, Marlys (Miller) Denholm,
Evelyn and Henry, Shirley (Gaber) Miller, and Nyla Miller.
Back row, John Dehnolm, David Miller, and Darrell Miller.

**Henry and Evelyn Miller and grandchildren,
Danny Miller, Tammie and Chris Denholm in 1961.**

**Evelyn Miller with grandchildren at Christmastime 1966.
Front row from left, Greg Miller, Lonnie Mandel,
Chris Denholm, Jim Miller, and Danny Miller.
Back row, Davey Miller and Tammie Denholm.**

**Danny Miller
and
Grandpa Henry
playing solitaire.**

**Lonnie and Vivian
Mandel with
Grandma and Grandpa
Miller in
September 1967.**

**Grandma and
Grandpa
Miller with
Tammie, Chris,
and Holli Denholm
in November 1967.**

Henry and Evelyn's children still enjoying
each other's company in December 1977.
Bet David said something funny!
David Miller, Marlys Denholm,
Darrell Miller, and Nyla Mandel.

Nyla Mandel,
Marlys Denholm,
and
Darrell Miller
together
in October 2015.

**Nyla Miller Mandel, Edna Miller Fields-Frerking,
and Marlys Miller Denholm gathered during the
funeral of Roy Frerking in Lemmon in the late 1990s.**

**Cousins Nyla Miller Mandel, Linda Holdal Hendricks,
Roberta Fields Brim and Marlys Miller Denholm
were together in the late 1990s.**

Marlys Miller Denholm

History
By Marlys Miller Denholm

August 1934 –
   Miss Evelyn Wampler of Hecla has been hired to teach at the Even School for the 1934-1935 school term. Miss Wampler is a graduate of the Northern Normal Institute (NNIS) at Aberdeen and holds a state certificate in primary education.

April 1936 –
   Mr. and Mrs. David Wampler of Hecla announce the engagement of their daughter, Evelyn, to Mr. Henry Miller of Lemmon. Miss Wampler is teaching near Thunder Hawk, and Mr. Miller is in sheep ranching.

June 1936 –
Wampler-Miller vows exchanged at McIntosh
   Evelyn Wampler of Hecla and Henry Miller of Lemmon were united in marriage on June 1, at 2 p.m. in the home of the Rev. Otto Lohse at MacIntosh. The Rev. Lohse performed the ceremony. Attendants were Mr. and Mrs. Fred (Hilda) Baumeister of Lemmon; brother-in-law and sister of the groom. The bride has been teaching near Thunder Hawk and the groom is engaged in sheep ranching south of Lemmon.

-Part C-
TO FINISH THE STORY
BY MARLYS MILLER DENHOLM
(1979)

I didn't meet my dad until a couple weeks before his thirty-seventh birthday, so would share a few stories told to me.

My dad farmed what was called the hay farm, then in the mid-1930s he went to work herding sheep for Tom Duncan south of McIntosh and Keldron, South Dakota.

About now, Evelyn Wampler found her way to a teaching job at the Even School near Keldron. Mother came from the Hecla area, the third daughter of David and Anna (Dinger) Wampler. After two years of college and several terms of teaching in the rural schools of Brown County, she moved west.

Mother has told how she stayed in Hecla to go to high school and that her father would bring eggs and cream to sell on Friday. Mother would ride home atop a load of coal or supplies to spend a weekend or vacation with the family. This included Ethel Ladner, Edith Erwin, Robert Wampler, Mother, Kenneth Wampler, and Edna Clark.

As a child, Mother attended the Dunkard or Dutch Reformed Church in the local school. In later years there was a Methodist church in Detroit Township. My grandparents and many older relatives are in that cemetery. The building was moved to Webster some years ago where it serves the Assembly of God congregation.

* * * * *

In the western schools the teacher often lived in the building, but a few places furnished a small cottage. Mother once walked a mile or so to spend the evening with friends and on her return to the creaky school building, she found a large black cat peering at her from the top of a bookcase. Mother took the broom and showed the animal the door.

When she told others, they said it was a wonder the cat hadn't attacked. After that, she didn't leave the door open, no matter what the weather. The next caller might be a skunk or a rattlesnake!

One young couple who befriended Mother were a Mr. and Mrs. Glass who are the parents of Rev. Bill Glass who served in Aberdeen some years ago. Our parents kept in touch with the elder Glasses for years.

One term, or part of it, Mother's sister, Edna, whom we knew as "Aunt Sally", stayed at the school with her. The sisters always called each other by the names "Sally" and "Sara," though none of the rest of the family used the nicknames. As children, they had read a story of a girl whose name was Sally. Mother had teasingly called her sister "Sally" and Aunt Edna said if she was a Sally then Mother was a Sara. And that's how it was.

It was a great comfort to have company at the school. The large noisy buildings had no shades or curtains and only a small kerosene lamp to dispel the shadows. Furniture and floors creaked and moaned as the day cooled and darkened. Shingles and chimneys have a way of becoming noisy after dark. The girls' living quarters were in a corner where they kept house and tried to make it homey. Wages were $50 a month.

Teachers would hike quite long distances to spend a weekend together. One spring two or three of the young teachers hitch-hiked to Aberdeen for Easter. They hid money in their stockings and "hit the road." They got rides and had no trouble with anyone, but even then it wasn't an entirely safe thing to do. Trains ran east and west at the time, but this was cheaper and an adventure. Mother and her friends took the train back to the schools after vacation.

The Even School building was the scene of neighborhood card parties and dances, just as in the days of homesteading.

Henry Miller showed up at one of the get-togethers. He wore the old-style high heeled cowboy boots, and Miss Wampler thought he was "a tall man, not a medium one." By the time she found out, it didn't make any difference. He became a regular party goer, and soon asked if he might drop in sometime.

On one occasion, Dad brought some "Oh, Henry" candy bars. The wrappers were dropped into the large wastebasket that stood near the teacher's desk. Naturally the children spotted them, and at recess began to chant, "Oh, Henry! Oh, Henry!" And my mother was an easily embarrassed person!

Once a packrat or such rodent stole Mother's comb and she was forced to "comb" her hair with her fingers until she could get to town to buy another. Does one tell one's man friend and have him think her a poor housekeeper? Or does one say nothing and hope he won't wonder about her grooming habits?

The summer of 1935, Mother spent with her family in Brown County, and Dad made a trip to Yellowstone Park and Washington State with Lee Edwards, a Mr. Backman and a couple of Ford boys. They toured a mine and a lumber camp and mill, but decided against working there. In Washington they camped and thinned apples and picked berries to restore their finances. Dad enjoyed these jobs and told us years later about it and the trip. Later they worked on a sugar beet farm and on a dairy and lettuce ranch. The trip west was one of the high points of Dad's life, and he told us of it for many years.

After harvest, Dad returned to Lemmon and Keldron. School was in session, and he had something to say to the teacher.

When Mother was taken to meet the Millers, she got an odd impression of her future father-in-law. The family was sitting on the porch after the noon meal when someone spotted a cow on the road. My grandma and a couple of the younger children went after the animal while Grandpa sat in his rocking chair calling, "Run, Mamas, run!"

He probably was simply cheering her along, but Mother's father would not have sat rocking and smoking while his wife ran after a cow! Mother found a close friend in sister-in-law, Clara, also a teacher. Dad's little sisters and Don were teenagers, and Mother found a houseful of friends in all the family. Grandma and Hilda were always some of her favorite people, too.

Evelyn Wampler and Henry Miller were married at McIntosh on June 1, 1935. Fred and Hilda Baumeister were their attendants. The folks gathered up Mother's things at the school and headed east. They spent a day or two in Aberdeen, then went to the Wampler farm south and east of Hecla. They arrived late at night and rather than disturb the family, rolled bedding onto the ground under a row of majestic cottonwoods in the yard.

In the morning, as my grandmother took her customary walk to the outhouse in the backyard, Mother called, "Good morning!" I can well imagine my grandmother's consternation at having campers watch her take her morning walk! So the Wamplers met their cowboy son-in-law. My dad loved both Gram and Gramp, and as far as I know he was always on good terms with all the family.

Dad didn't care for the flat land here; he said he felt as though he were in a hole and looking uphill.

One thing Dad liked to tell was how surprised he was when he and Mother drove out to see Mother's black mare, Susie. Our mother and Uncle Ken Wampler had raised and trained the colt, a crossbred they had gotten from Dr. Rice's racing stables near Britton. These were trotters, so it is safe to guess they were Standardbreds.

Dad said, "She took a bridle and walked out and called, 'Come, Susie.' The mare came right up to her and your mother put the bridle on and grabbed a handful of hair and swung up. Then she galloped around bareback! And I stood with my mouth hanging open." Where he came from, you run, chase, rope and tie a horse; then if you're lucky and in practice, you can ride him.

Susie was a good kid- and cattle-pony, and she lived until 1955. When I was about eleven, Dad fell over some toys on the porch and hurt an elbow. Then he needed some emergency herding done, and asked if I could take Susie to bring up the animals. He said, "Just show her what you want to do and hang on, she'll take care of it." I thought he was fooling. He wasn't. I showed her what I wanted to do, and she did it, and I hung on. I have had great respect for cutting horses and their trainers ever since!

Western South Dakota was in the drought of 1936, and my folks drove to Turton, South Dakota, to make arrangements to ship my Grandfather Miller's cattle there for the winter. The livestock were unloaded from the train at Groton and herded south by horsemen. From what I have heard it was a very bad winter. The poor, weakened cattle sickened and many died. Mother went to Aberdeen to try to find work, but no one was hiring married women.

Once the folks ran out of flour and when a cow died, my dad sold the skin for enough money for a small sack of much-needed flour. They soaked whole wheat in hot water each evening and cooked that for breakfast cereal. By spring, Mother was expecting and how she craved apples and oranges! But there were none to be had even if there'd been money for them.

In the spring, the remaining cattle were sold and my parents took a job of driving a herd of horses to Lemmon. Uncle Bill Miller had come east with the cattle, and he went with my folks to help. Mother brought the car and they camped and cooked out nights along the way. The trip done, Uncle Bill returned to the Conde area where he lived out his life except for some years in Europe during WWII. He passed away in January 1974.

We (by then I was in evidence) moved back to Hecla where my dad drove a truck for Uncle Curt Erwin who was married to Mother's sister, Edith. Dad left for work one morning and returned that eve to find himself a father.

The next winter or two we lived in a sheep herder's wagon in Corson County and Dad again worked for the Duncans. I don't remember them, but my folks thought a great deal of Tom and Dora Duncan and their children. I have a lovely old plate the Duncans gave the folks as a wedding gift. It has always been the "birthday cake plate."

I don't remember the herder's wagon as a home, but I remember it as a summer camp. My mother insisted that the wagon home be set facing north for the summer. She said it would be cooler. There was some grumbling about "Hank's woman" but the wagon was set as she wished. Soon all the herders were facing their wagons away from the summer's heat and flies.

In 1940, we moved to a farm south of Shadehill. This was a grain and cattle farm, and the folks milked quite a few cows. Here we had an irrigated garden. One summer Dad built frames and covered them with screening to save the tomatoes from the grasshoppers. The beasts dug under the wood and ate the plants! We did get a better car and a ringer washing machine while we lived there.

Women in my grandparents' generation were lucky if they had sewing machines, and it is said that my Grandma Miller treasured hers. Women of my mother's generation grew up expecting they would have sewing machines, and Mother bought one before she was married. But to her, the washing machine with a gas engine was a most valued helper.

The Christmas I was three, we got baby brother and a tricycle. That spring we moved to south of Athboy in Corson County, and Dad raised sheep on shares with Walter Parrot. We lived in a three-room house and our dad took the sheep herder's wagon out on the range only in the summer.

This was far from Lemmon, roads were less than good, and the car stood on blocks in the winter. We went into Lemmon for overnight at Thanksgiving and brought home car and trailer loaded with the winter's provisions. From then until spring thaw and flooding were past, team and hay sled or wagon were basic transportation.

From A Soddy

We stayed home! We never had any bad accidents, fires or illnesses. We were taught to be very careful in all such matters. The mail was brought once a week or less often depending on the weather. Our parents ordered the Sunday school papers right from the publishing house, and how we enjoyed them and the letters from the family! I remember getting Valentines from the Ladner cousins and what a treat that was.

We did have a flood one spring after Dad had gone out on the range. Gram Wampler and Aunt Ethel were there. Mother loaded us all in the car and dashed across the spot where water was already over the trail. We spent a day or two at the boss' house a couple miles away. Then someone rode over to our place and came back to say the water hadn't reached the house and it was safe to go home. The hens had had a hard time of it as the chicken coop was a dug-out along the creek bank. The poor birds had to stay on the roosts for a couple of days while the flooding creek went down.

Once three-year-old David locked himself in the car and took a nap. Later he was discovered howling and panicky. Mother tried for some time to show him how to pull the little button to open the door, but he only cried more. Fearing he would collapse, she took a tool and cracked a window. Before she finished breaking in, Davey opened the door and was rescued. A thermometer set the car quickly zoomed to 120 degrees.

One summer when our dad was out with the flock of sheep, a predator began taking the half-grown chicks. So Mother set some traps. In the morning she had caught a young skunk which she killed with a hammer. Dad had with him the only firearm, a single shot .22, and Mother would not have used it had she had it.

The next day the trap held the mother skunk! This one our mother killed with the ax. I've never known how one does that without the skunk getting in a few licks, but as far as I know, Mother avoided that.

Mother knew where to find Dad and the flock, so one Easter we went out to the wagon. A sheep herder's wagon was about the size of a hayrack. This one was on rubber tires and was moved by the tractor so the eveners were gone. Inside it was the same as ever, the tiny stove near the Dutch door, a table hinged to the wall, one or two chairs, double doors to reveal a storage area under the bed that filled the back third of the single room under a rounded roof.

We children slept on the floor and in the morning hunted the colored eggs out amidst the singing of the larks and the blatting of the sheep as they moved out for the day. Soon Dad had to follow the herd, we packed up and went home. This has always been a special Easter to me!

When I started to school, Mother and we children and our Aunt Edith Erwin moved to what was called the Bronson School south the Grand River. We lived in a small cottage and our aunt kept the little folks during the day. Each night she and I took a flashlight and crossed the dark, windy yard to our sleeping quarters in the school building. Dad spent the winter with the dogs, sheep and hay team. He came to the school for the Christmas program and little Nyla had forgotten him. She cried for our aunt to take her. We and Mother then went to spend the vacation at the ranch with Dad.

Back at school we faced the winter of 1943-44. The school didn't have a well and with the deep snow, we couldn't go after water, so our aunt and mother melted tubs of snow for all purposes and boiled the water for us to drink. One time Mother went to get coal from a shed and there, curled up and sound asleep, was a big skunk. We had to have coal, so Mother quietly filled the pails and left. The next time she went for coal the animal was gone.

The Joe Wiesingers lived east of the school. They loaded a car on some kind of sled and pulled it with a four-horse team past the school, out to the highway so they could get into Lemmon. The men picked up mail and groceries for the few folks living out there. We watched them go past and I remember how the horses steamed in the cold air. One of the men came to the door to ask if we wanted to mail anything and if we had a grocery order. Mother ordered a case of canned milk.

Somehow when the groceries were brought, the case of milk was left at the neighbor's farm a mile or more away at the highway. In a few days our mother had to walk that long mile after a day of teaching and carry home a few cans of milk. This she did every other day or until someone went along with a team and sled again.

When spring came, it was so muddy that we had to walk to a neighboring farm to carry water back to the school, as the road was impassable. Teachers were getting $100 a month, and our mother saved enough so we could take the train to Aberdeen and Hecla that summer to visit relatives.

Dad had quit training broncs, but he liked dogs and he had some well-trained sheep dogs. I recall a white female he was proud of and another called Teddy. Once when we visited him on the range, our dad called the dog and pointed way off at a hill. "Get 'em!" The dog ran around the flock and chased some coyotes up the hill and into their den. Dad didn't like us to play with his working dogs.

In 1944, Dad sold his share of the flock and bought a farm, the only farm I think he ever owned. This was in DeWitte Township just a mile south of the old Miller homestead site, which then was in government pasture. Our new home was near the Miller school, and our mother taught there three years. Uncle Louie's family lived across the section east and a bit south, and we were allowed to walk or ride horseback to play with our cousins. Our dad and uncle farmed together.

We older ones could ride so we could bring up the cows and "watch fences." Our dad was a natural teacher and was always teaching in the way he talked or did something. He didn't tell us not to forget or that we needed to know or make a big deal of it. But after a while, you'd see that what he'd said was worth knowing. Years later when I should have known better, I raced the old pony and let her get too warm. I took care of her and she didn't even get stiff. I was into my 20s when I told Dad. His comment? "It's a good thing I told you how to cool a horse."

******

Grandma Miller was this kind of teacher. Grandpa had a different way. One of the first things I remember about him was his "false teeth." He'd pull them out and ask if we could do that. "Ach!" Grandma would snort, "They don't want to see your old teeth!"

Grandpa laughed at her. He didn't try to remember our names. I don't think he was sure who we all belonged to. Grandpa called the girls "Sissy" and the boys "Bubby."

Like Grandpa, Dad rarely laid a hand on us. We probably averaged two spankings each. Dad didn't have to spank. He had a quiet way of making you wish you'd done differently. Long practice as the oldest of the family had trained him to mediate children's arguments, and both parties were usually satisfied and learned something. Dad was fair and patient with us, even when we did some pretty stupid things.

Our dad was careful with the animals, but he did have a runway once with a corn binder. He had stopped to make an adjustment and the center horse hooked his bridle on something. The old leather gave way and the three-horse team left. Dad knew they would circle toward the slowest horse, and that was right back to the barn. When he left, the little children had been playing in a gateway nearby. Poor Dad ran stumbling across the corn rows, calling for the children to get into the hay yard ahead of the team.

The kids moved to safety and the corn binder hooked a corner post, bringing the runaway to a grinding halt and letting pigs out all over the place.

One Christmas in the 1940s Uncle Bill Miller came home to Lemmon. He and my dad got to talking about the people in the Conde/Turton area, and next thing Bill was saying that the people he worked for needed a man on one of their places.

From A Soddy

Things began to move, and that winter the folks sold out to
Louie and we were getting ready to move to Day County where
Dad would work for the Taylor brothers. This was an easy
move for my mother as we would be about fifty miles south
and east of Hecla, where most of her family lived.

Our dad moved his work horses, tractor and some household
things in April and we stayed to finish the school term. Dad
wrote that there was still snow piled high along the roads in
April 1948. We hadn't had a hard winter in Perkins County.
When school was out, we all moved, and the next winter the
Perkins County folks suffered a hard winter.

In Day County we went to a larger school. Our first teacher
is now Pastor Loren Espland. We had a good 4-H in Scotland
Township and the American Union kept up rural Sunday
schools. We soon became part of the community. The Lester
Smiths befriended us and they were some of my folks' best
friends long after both couples had left the area. Other good
friends were the Millard Denholms, who later became my
parents-in-law.

There was running water and electricity at the Taylor farm
to make Dad's work easier. Once he had time, so he made a
batch of doughnuts and we took some to school in our lunches.
It caused quite a stir when we said our dad had made them. He
liked to make bread, too. Dad had been a bachelor so much that
he had learned to cook quite well. He didn't criticize our
mother's cooking, nor did he cook if there was a good-sized
girl who could do it. He did make the best fudge!

Our folks liked the farm, the business arrangement, and the
neighbors at south Andover. It was a blow when Taylors
cancelled the contract. I never did know why, and I don't know
if the folks did. Maybe it was the Lord's way of moving us, as
my brother David was having more and more trouble with
asthma. He was hospitalized each fall we lived there.

We moved to a Falkstad farm west of Bristol, and in the
higher elevation, David was much better.

We went to Bristol School where we all graduated. Dad farmed the way he had for years, using the tractor for big jobs and his horses for haying, corn planting and cultivating. Mother taught school. Our parents transferred to the Methodist church, and when our turns came, we also became members. Dad took the instruction course, and it sparked his interest in religious literature. Dad was far from ignorant in spite of his lack of formal schooling. He spent winter evenings reading books, magazines, papers and pamphlets. I never saw him actively reading the Bible, but he read a lot of prophesy material and he knew what it said.

Our folks didn't talk about religion. They talked about what was fair, what was honest and what was the right thing to do or the way to act or behave. We knew what was expected of us.

My early childhood vision of being "in God's hands" made me think of a baby chick in my father's cupped hands, safe and protected and peeking out. Couldn't we all use a little of that?

One thing I especially remember from my teens was our parents going over the sermon with us at Sunday dinner. We were asked questions, offered insights, invited to express our thoughts, and in general helped to see how the message might be applied to our own lives. It was years before I realized how great this was.

Mother taught school and then came home to kids and work. She did her school work late at night. Once Dad grumbled because she let the fire die down and sat on the desk to keep her feet warm while she checked papers. Our mother taught for seven years before she married and for ten while I was in school. She then topped this off with five more years before she retired.

My parents' concern for the children of others was extended to my cousin, Bob, who lived with us for several years off and on. When he was lost in Korea, we felt we had lost a brother. Later, age and health wouldn't allow live-in foster care, but the folks aided some American Indian children through "Save the

Children." They never saw the youngsters, but sent cards and letters and contributed to their care.

We always planted a garden right after school was out. Housecleaning, painting or papering followed, and then canning, and sewing in time for school. One summer we raised 300 hen-hatched chicks and turkeys!

Cars were a frustration to Dad and he never did much tinkering. When he sold his share of the Taylor cattle, Dad decided, "If we never have anything again, we are going to have a new car once." He got a Plymouth, and several years later hit a cow and ruined the car. The one he got then lasted him the rest of his life. Dad had fun with the boys when they worried about starting cars. He'd say his never failed him. Finally, Darrell said, "Well, you don't start it unless it's forty-five degrees or better." Dad laughed. That was so, but his car hadn't failed him.

Louie says my dad had "a way" with animals, but "could get tough." Dad's last chore team was a lanky old sorrel mare we rode some and a chunky black that he said would have been a good roping horse. One morning in the 1950s, Dad led the team to water when the black was feeling his oats. Fritz reached over and nipped Dad's arm, bringing blood. Without a word, Dad picked up a neck yoke and slapped the gelding in the head. Fritz collapsed. "Hope I killed you," Dad growled, examining his arm. The horse got up and shook himself, and they went about the day's work.

This same horse, a couple years earlier, fell on ice and slipped into the water tank. Fritz was stuck with his legs folded under his body. Quietly and patiently, Dad worked for over an hour to free the wet and frightened animal without the tank being broken or either of them getting hurt.

Dad was gentle with the babies. I have seen him cuddle a baby chick or duck in both hands and talk to it, calling it a "little fella." He enjoyed the lambs and called all the ewes, "Betsy."

I suspect the 1950-57 years were hard for our parents. For one thing, we were all teenagers and our folks were not young.

We had work to do, but we also had the opportunity to be in band and some sports.

Grandma Wampler passed away the summer of 1953, and both Gramp and Uncle Rob the next year. Mother's health began to fail at about this time.

In December of 1955, when I was in college, Mom, Dad, Uncle Bill, and I made the trip to Lemmon when Grandpa Miller passed on. In January, our mother was hospitalized with pneumonia and extreme fatigue. She had been doing two peoples' work for too long! She was in and out of the hospital for most of the winter. We girls did the housework, laundry, and baking when I was home on Saturday. (Yes, bread, too.)

Once I suggested to Dad that I drop out of school. I could go the summer and have my certificate to teach. Dad almost broke down; he insisted that I stay in school. I might be needed more come summer. A year or more later, he told Darrell and me that the doctor hadn't known whether our mother would live. Dad never burdened us with this, but worked and worried and prayed alone. After this illness our mother was plagued with asthma, but by being careful and resting often, she lived a near normal life for 13 years.

In the 1950s, we got Dad a harmonica for his birthday. He could still play one! He claimed to be a poor player, but we thought he was good. Dad had been quite a dancer in his prime, and he still enjoyed music, though he said flatly he "couldn't carry a tune in a paper sack." Dad went to the games when we were in school; he liked the visiting and the band.

One time it happened that we four youngsters went alone, and it was bitterly cold. On the way home we got off the road and got stuck a mile west of Bristol. We walked over to George Wattier's and spent the night. There was no phone at either place, so we couldn't let the folks know we were safe. What a night they must have had!

In the morning, Mr. Wattier and Darrell walked into town and got someone to start the car and get it on the road. It was around nine when we got home. Dad was finishing chores and

Mother was mixing bread. We told what had happened, and as I remember, they didn't scold or make a fuss. They believed us and trusted our judgement.

If our parents had ethnic, racial or religious prejudices, they kept them well hidden. I was surprised when I was about sixteen to hear Dad say many of the older Germans had left the homeland because the Jews were getting so strong.

We were not allowed to poke fun at anyone's way or troubles. When I was in the lower grades we were talking about a fat lady and our mother said, we might be like that one day. Once we mimicked some children who had a speech problem and Dad snapped, "Don't do that! Any one of you could have been born like that."

Dad usually kept scolding or correction private. But when we were in our young teens, one of my brothers decided to go to town in dirty work clothes on Saturday night. After a couple of occurrences, Dad asked why he was doing this.

"They'll think I'm tough," my brother explained.

"They'll think you're a pig," Dad corrected. That's still funny.

The spring of 1957, Dad went to work for Hansmeier and Sons Farms of Bristol. The next ten years were some of his happiest. He was relieved of the worries of farming for one's self, but he was out on the land and doing the work he loved.

Dad enjoyed visiting with the late Henry Hansmeier who had come from Germany in his youth. Dad found that he could understand some of the language, but speaking was another matter.

Dad spoke well of the Hansmeier boys, then in high school. He said they treated the men with courtesy and respect, did their share and never acted like they were anybody special. That meant a lot to him.

In about 1964, Dad began working part-time and choosing the nice weather seasons. He was proud to have worked the whole season of 1967.

Our parents had their own home in east Bristol, good friends and neighbors and few family responsibilities. During these years they made several short trips to visit relatives in the Dakotas and western Minnesota. My husband, John Denholm, and I made the folks grandparents in 1958, an honor they enjoyed. They lived to see nine grandchildren.

When several of us would be there on a Sunday, Dad would ask us to play whist. We hadn't played as youngsters as he couldn't teach the lot of us at once. He certainly enjoyed giving us a drubbing now! When the game of Scrabble came along, both Dad and Mom got into it. One of Dad's good friends was the late Ernest March. What a pair of teasers and jokers they were! We could hardly play a game with them; they made up words, spelled phonetically, and had so much fun that the game was all but lost. I think the bull in the haymow story of the 1920s is one of Ernest's, as no one in the family seems to recall it.

******

Late in the fall of 1967, Dad began having what he called stomach trouble. The doctor put him on an ulcer diet. In February of 1968, he went into the hospital for gall bladder surgery. The doctors found a large tumor they dared not touch. Our dad rallied for a couple of weeks and there was some talk of radium treatments. Then he began to fail and told us he "knew what he was up against."

For a month, our Dad waved to grandchildren at the window, kept interested in the activities of the family, and let Mother read him the paper. He chose not to go on intravenous feeding and rarely asked for anything for pain.

Members of the family made the trip to visit, and this prompted Dad to joke, "I must be in bad shape. Everyone's coming to see me!"

Our mother hardly ever went to Webster in the evening, but she did that April 16. Darrell and his wife, Jan, were there when Dad took a bad turn. We came and hurried through the familiar halls of the small hospital. We had been in and out for two months; there was no doubt as to who we were or why we were there, yet no one stopped us. We went to Dad's room, expecting to find the family.

The bed was empty and the bedding rolled back! The room was bright and relieved of pain and gloom, the air was different. There was no one there, but "He is not here. He is risen!" seemed to sing in the air. Relief, the ordeal was over; joy, the Lord had taken him. Is this how the women at the tomb felt? How far from empty room to empty tomb? How far from death to life?

Someone showed us to the family room where we joined Mother, Darrell and Jan, and our pastor, Glen Phillips. I asked Mother if she was all right. She said, "I'm so relieved!" Grief had been and loneliness would come, but for now she thanked God.

We feared for our mother's health, but she held up well for more than a year. During this time she visited friends and family. She kept up a car and drove to my youngest sibling, Nyla's, to stay with the children while Nyla worked.

Then a change in doctors brought a change in medicine. Mother began to fail and was gone in a month. July 20, 1969, we went fishing and listened to the first moon landing on the radio and came back to find the family at her home. Mother had died so suddenly, and she was the only one who knew where we were. Darrell and Janice had come and found her.

It is not my intention to end on a sad note. We have family and friends, memories, God's love and Jesus' promise. Someone asked if it wasn't hard to sell the folks' things. Jan said that we had taken the things we wanted and "anyway things weren't important to Darrell's parents. How people were treated and what was said to each other were the things they valued."

Is this an unusual story? No. There are millions like it, thousands of them recorded, at least hundreds told better. The more I study the history of our state, the more I wonder if it was courage, greed or foolhardiness that drove so many to try homesteading. All of those born at the turn of the century and living into the Space Age have lived in unusual times. Each era has at some time been unusual. We seem to feel a need to sift through history, looking for something worth saving and trying to incorporate it into our lives. We hope you have enjoyed this look back in time to one family's journey to the prairie.

This is a copy of a check Dad had written out to pay the winter fuel oil bill in 1966. Note his beautiful handwriting, even with his advancing age.

From A Soddy

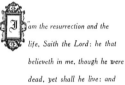

"am the resurrection and the
life, Saith the Lord: he that
believeth in me, though he were
dead, yet shall he live: and
whosoever liveth and believeth
in me, shall never die."

John 11 — 25:26

In Remembrance

CASKET BEARERS

ACTIVE

Andrew Brandlee
Raymond Loterbauer
Robert Schneider
Robert Loterbauer
Willie Korf
Bert Mauritzson

HONORARY

Ernest March
Lester Smith
Fred Dauwen
Millard Denholm
Ralph Hansmeier
Wallace Moore

IN MEMORY OF
Henry Ernest Miller
August 30, 1900 · April 16, 1968

SERVICES
2:00 p. m. Friday, April 19, 1968
First Methodist Church
Bristol, S. Dak.

CLERGY
Rev. Glenn W. Phillips
Webster, S. Dak.

INTERMENT
Scotland Cemetery
Crandall, S. Dak.

Funeral Arrangements by
FIKSDAL FUNERAL SERVICE
Webster, S. Dak.

Marlys Miller Denholm

-Epilogue-

BY MARLYS MILLER DENHOLM
(2016)

The original *From a Soddy* sold out in only a couple of years. I was surprised when my daughter, Holli Seehafer, asked to republish her grandfather's pioneer account. Holli is an author in her own right, having some Christian romances in print. Holli asked for an epilogue – is that a follow-up?

Most of the people mentioned in *Soddy*, of course, are gone. Grandpa William (Bill) Miller died in December of 1955, having reached the age of 86. Grandma Carrie Lang Miller died in May of 1960 at the age of 79 and one-half. Both are buried at the Lemmon Cemetery south of town. They lived to see 29 grandchildren, I believe.

Their children included:

Christoff Miller, their firstborn, July 1899-fall 1913. He was named for his paternal grandfather, Christoff Meuller, as was the German custom. He is buried in the Lemmon, SD, cemetery.

Henry Ernest Miller, August 1900-April 1968. He was named for his maternal grandfather, Henry Lang. Henry married Evelyn Wampler (March 1910-July 1969) of Hecla, SD. She had gone west to teach school. They raised a family of four, including Marlys Miller Denholm, Darrell Miller, David Miller (deceased), and Nyla Miller Mandel. Henry and Evelyn are buried in the Scotland Cemetery south of Andover, SD.

Hilda Hannah Miller Baumeister, July 1903-August 1983. She married Fred Baumeister and raised six children. They included Vern, Gene (deceased), Lyle (deceased), Neal, Joanne, and Leone. Hilda and Fred are buried at Lemmon, SD.

Louie Charles Miller, September 1905-April 1988. He married Clara Hoefling, who was a teacher, and they raised four children. Their children included Arlene, Duane, Loren, and Shirley (deceased). Louie passed away on the twentieth anniversary of Henry's death. Louie and Clara are buried at Lemmon, SD.

Walter Miller. Died at birth and was buried near Pipestone, MN, before the family moved to Lemmon, SD.

William (Bill) F. Miller, October 1909-February 1974. Uncle Bill was the first of the family born on the homestead at Lemmon, SD. He never married. He was a World War II veteran who served through four consecutive Christmases during the war. After his discharge, he lived and died at Conde, SD. He is buried at Scotland Cemetery south of Andover, SD.

Lester Miller, 1910-1993. He was a World War II veteran. He married Inga Thompson and they moved to Idaho. They had no children, and are buried near Coeur D' Alene, ID.

Edward Miller, 1911-1921. He died after an injury, as was depicted in Uncle Louie's chapter of the book. Edward is buried in the Lemmon, SD, cemetery.

Ella Miller Texley, 1914-1989. She married Mike Texley and raised a family of six. Their children included Bob (deceased), Beverly, Carol, Marvin, Dennis, and Jerry.

Donald Miller, 1916-1990. He married Bea Ashmore in mid-life and gained some grown stepchildren. Don is buried at Lemmon, SD.

Edna Caroline Miller Fields Frerking, November 1919-2012. She married Bob Fields from Lemmon. They were a military family and raised two children – Roberta and Terry (deceased). After Edna was widowed, she married Roy Frerking of Lemmon. They lived in Arizona but are buried at Lemmon.

Alice Miller Holdal, July 1921-December 1988. Married Emmett Holdal and they raised seven children. They were

Gary, Linda, Deryl, Joyce, Johnny, Rhonda, and Rodney. My Dad, Henry, as late as the 1950s, introduced Alice as his baby sister, and she exclaimed, "Some things you never outgrow!" George Miller, 1922-1923. He was not a healthy baby and his life was short. He is buried at the Lemmon Cemetery.

After my parents and grandparents were gone, the aunts kept in touch by mail and occasional visits. The dear ladies! Aunt Clara, who married into the family, told me – "Dear little grandma (her mother-in-law) had thirteen live births and Lord knows how many miscarriages."

My family, or my children and I, made the 250 mile trip from Bristol, where we lived, to Lemmon a number of times. My sister, Nyla, and I have been "out west" as well. She was only five years old when we moved to Day County, so perhaps she isn't as "attached" to the family at Lemmon.

A little more information about Henry and Evelyn's children and grandchildren follows.

I, Marlys, am the oldest. I was born in 1937. I married John Denholm of Andover, SD, in 1957. We have two daughters, Tammie Denholm and Holli Seehafer, and a son, Chris Denholm. We have six grandchildren and ten great-grandchildren.

Darrell Edward Miller was born in May 1939. He married Janice Jiran of Bristol and the couple raised three children. They are Gregory Miller, Jim Miller and Kathy Kwasniewski. Janice passed away in 1994. Darrell has seven grandchildren.

David William Miller was born in December 1940. He married Shirley Gabor of Bristol, and later married Donna Johnson of Minneapolis. He raised two sons, David and Daniel, and two stepsons, Chris and Carl. David passed away in 2003.

Nyla June Miller was born in June 1942. She married Jerome Mandel of Doland, SD. They raised two sons, Lonnie and Rick, and a daughter, Vivian Mulder. Nyla and Jerry have six grandchildren and four great-grandchildren.

The following is a brief summarization regarding some of my dad's relatives after the *Soddy* was published in 1979. My dad knew that his Aunt Tina Lang had moved to Canada to homestead there. He assumed that she had died and was buried in Canada. In 1982, my family traveled to Lemmon for the city's 75th anniversary celebration, and Alice and Emmet Holdal's 40th wedding anniversary. While there, I met my dad's Aunt Tina, who obviously was still alive – apparently some family members had stayed in touch. She and one of her granddaughters had come down for the celebrations as well. Tina bought a copy of *From a Soddy*.

A short time later, I received a letter from Tina's daughter, Lena Ellingson, telling me her mother had suddenly slipped away and is buried at Radville, Saskatchewan Canada. The community is located about 15 miles north of the Montana and North Dakota border. Lena Ellingson and I exchanged Christmas cards until 2014.

My dad's Aunt Mary Lang married a Mr. Reedy. In the 1950s she traveled from Minnesota by train to Washington or Oregon. In transit, she stopped for a visit in Lemmon. My dad saw her a few times when they were both in Lemmon.

Mary's son, Ed, lived on the east coast, and my parents kept up correspondence with him and his wife, Mary. After my parents' passing, I exchanged Christmas cards with Ed and Mary a few years. The couple stopped to visit me at Bristol when they were en route west in the 1980s.

Dad's cousin, Elsie Graphenteen, was along back in Dad's 1920 story about the relatives who visited the road crew camp. She was the daughter of Dad's Aunt Anna and Charles Graphenteen of Pipestone, MN. As an adult, Elsie married Everett Hatfield and they lived at Ortonville, MN.

When my parents lived at Bristol, they visited the Hatfields a number of times. After my parents' passing, we kept up correspondence as long as the Hatfields lived. My son, Chris, and I drove from Bristol to attend the celebration of Elsie and Everett's 50th anniversary. Also, Louie and Clara Miller drove to Ortonville along with their daughter, Arlene, and son-in-law, Ernest Kari, from Perkins County.

In about 1970, Aunt Hilda Baumeister came on the bus to Bristol, and we drove over to Ortonville and spent a few days with Elsie and Everett. One day Elsie drove us to Pipestone, MN, to see her sister, Marie. Marie was Dad and Hilda's cousin.

On this same trip, we also saw another sister of Elsie's – I believe she was Rose. She had worked in a school kitchen, and on a stormy day, someone had hit her car and broken her arm. The arm had not healed correctly and had a bend in it, but she was pleasant and thankful that it was as good as it was.

Some years later I drove to Ortonville for Elsie's funeral.

In the story of the filing for the claims, a Mr. Wiesinger was mentioned. The Wiesinger family homesteaded south of the Millers, across the Grand River. My dad and the Wiesinger children, including Joe, were young people together. Joe Wiesinger's daughter, Azalia, and I started to school together in Perkins County in 1943. In adulthood, she lived in Mobridge, SD, and had two boys about the same age as my oldest daughter. Azalia and I met in Aberdeen, SD, a few times and kept up correspondence until her death.

Recently, Summerville, SD, has begun hosting the Hugh Glass Festival as a tourism draw. Summerville appeared on the map in the 1950s in the approximate area that had been Shadehill, SD. Summerville came into being after the completion of the Shadehill Dam on the Grand River. In *From a Soddy*, my dad retold the story of Hugh Glass and his harrowing encounter with a bear. My parents were friends with some relatives of Hugh Glass who lived in the area. The movie, *The Revenant*, starring Leonardo DiCaprio, was released in late 2015. The movie was loosely based on the Hugh Glass story.

P. 13

95915873R00153

Made in the USA
San Bernardino, CA
17 November 2018